W9-AOX-688

MYTHMAKER:
The Story of J.K. Rowling
Second Edition

WHO
WROTE
THAT?

LOUISA MAY ALCOTT

JANE AUSTEN

AVI

JUDY BLUME

BETSY BYARS

BEVERLY CLEARY

ROBERT CORMIER

BRUCE COVILLE

ROALD DAHL

CHARLES DICKENS

THEODOR GEISEL

WILL HOBBS

ANTHONY HOROWITZ

GAIL CARSON LEVINE

C.S. LEWIS

ANN M. MARTIN

L.M. MONTGOMERY

PAT MORA

WALTER DEAN MYERS

SCOTT O'DELL

BARBARA PARK

GARY PAULSEN

TAMORA PIERCE

EDGAR ALLAN POE

BEATRIX POTTER

PHILIP PULLMAN

MYTHMAKER:
   THE STORY OF
   J.K. ROWLING

MAURICE SENDAK

SHEL SILVERSTEIN

R.L. STINE

EDWARD L.
   STRATEMEYER

E.B. WHITE

LAURA INGALLS
   WILDER

LAURENCE YEP

JANE YOLEN

WHO WROTE THAT?

MYTHMAKER:
The Story of J.K. Rowling
Second Edition

Amy Sickels

Foreword by
Kyle Zimmer

CHELSEA HOUSE
PUBLISHERS
An imprint of Infobase Publishing

MYTHMAKER: The Story of J.K. Rowling, Second Edition

Chelsea House
An imprint of Infobase Publishing
132 West 31st Street
New York NY 10001

Library of Congress Cataloging-in-Publication Data
Sickels, Amy.
  Mythmaker : the story of J.K. Rowling / Amy Sickels. — 2nd ed.
    p. cm. — (Who wrote that?)
  Rev. ed. of: Mythmaker / by Charles J. Shields.1st ed. 2002.
  Includes bibliographical references and index.
  ISBN 978-0-7910-9632-1 (hardcover)
  1. Rowling, J. K—Juvenile literature. 2. Authors, English—20th century—Biography—Juvenile literature. 3. Potter, Harry (Fictitious character)—Juvenile literature. 4. Children's stories—Authorship—Juvenile literature. I. Shields, Charles J., 1951– Mythmaker. II. Title. III. Series.
  PR6068.O93Z884 2008
  823'.914—dc22
  [B]   2008001202

C.1

Table of Contents

FOREWORD BY
KYLE ZIMMER
PRESIDENT, FIRST BOOK   6

1 WILD ABOUT HARRY   11

2 "QUIET, FRECKLY, SHORT-SIGHTED"   21

3 HARRY APPEARS   31

4 HALF A SUITCASE OF STORIES   41

5 BIDDING WAR   51

6 A PHENOMENON IN PUBLISHING   67

7 BREAKING RECORDS   81

8 CREATING HARRY'S WORLD   91

9 HARRY'S PLACE IN CHILDREN'S LITERATURE   101

CHRONOLOGY   114

NOTES   116

WORKS BY J.K. ROWLING   121

POPULAR BOOKS   122

POPULAR CHARACTERS   124

MAJOR AWARDS   126

BIBLIOGRAPHY   127

FURTHER READING   130

INDEX   132

FOREWORD BY
KYLE ZIMMER
PRESIDENT, FIRST BOOK

HUMANITY IS POWERED by stories. From our earliest days as thinking beings, we employed every available tool to tell each other stories. We danced, drew pictures on the walls of our caves, spoke, and sang. All of this extraordinary effort was designed to entertain, recount the news of the day, explain natural occurrences—and then gradually to build religious and cultural traditions and establish the common bonds and continuity that eventually formed civilizations. Stories are the most powerful force in the universe; they are the primary element that has distinguished our evolutionary path.

Our love of the story has not diminished with time. Enormous segments of societies are devoted to the art of storytelling. Book sales in the United States alone topped $24 billion in 2006; movie studios spend fortunes to create and promote stories; and the news industry is more pervasive in its presence than ever before.

There is no mystery to our fascination. Great stories are magic. They can introduce us to new cultures or remind us of the nobility and failures of our own; inspire us to greatness or scare us to death; but above all, stories provide human insight on a level that is unavailable through any other source. In fact, stories connect each of us to the rest of humanity not just in our own time, but also throughout history.

This special magic of books is the greatest treasure that we can hand down from generation to generation. In fact, that spark in a child that comes from books became the motivation for the creation of my organization, First Book, a national literacy program with a simple mission: to provide new books to the most disadvantaged children. First Book has been at work in hundreds of communities for over a decade. Every year, children in need receive millions of books through our organization, and millions more are provided through dedicated literacy institutions across the United States and around the world. In addition, groups of people dedicate themselves tirelessly to working with children to share reading and stories in every imaginable setting from schools to the streets. Of course, this Herculean effort serves many important goals. Literacy translates to productivity and employability in life and many other valid and even essential elements. But at the heart of this movement are people who love stories, love to read, and want desperately to ensure that no one misses the wonderful possibilities that reading provides.

When thinking about the importance of books, there is an overwhelming urge to cite the literary devotion of great minds. Some have written of the magnitude of the importance of literature. Amy Lowell, an American poet, captured the concept when she said, "Books are more than books. They are the life, the very heart and core of ages past, the reason why men lived and worked and died, the essence and quintessence of their lives." Others have spoken of their personal obsession with books, as in Thomas Jefferson's simple statement: "I live for books." But more compelling, perhaps, is the almost instinctive excitement in children for books and stories.

Throughout my years at First Book, I have heard truly extraordinary stories about the power of books in the lives of children. In one case, a homeless child, who had been bounced from one location to another, later resurfaced—and the only possession that he had fought to keep was the book he was given as part of a First Book distribution months earlier. More recently, I met a child who, upon receiving the book he wanted, flashed a big smile and said, "This is my big chance!" These snapshots reveal the true power of books and stories to give hope and change lives.

As these children grow up and continue to develop their love of reading, they will owe a profound debt to those volunteers who reached out to them—a debt that they may repay by reaching out to spark the next generation of readers. But there is a greater debt owed by all of us—a debt to the storytellers, the authors, who have bound us together, inspired our leaders, fueled our civilizations, and helped us put our children to sleep with their heads full of images and ideas.

WHO WROTE THAT? is a series of books dedicated to introducing us to a few of these incredible individuals. While we have almost always honored stories, we have not uniformly honored storytellers. In fact, some of the most important authors have toiled in complete obscurity throughout their lives or have been openly persecuted for the uncomfortable truths that they have laid before us. When confronted with the magnitude of their written work, we can forget that writers are people. They struggle through the same daily indignities and dental appointments, and they experience the intense joy and bottomless despair that many of us do. Yet, somehow they rise above it all to weave a powerful thread that connects us all. It is a rare honor to have the opportunity that these books provide to share the lives of these extraordinary people. Enjoy.

J.K. Rowling poses in the "Hogwarts Express" during a four-day promotional tour through Britain for Harry Potter and the Goblet of Fire. *The phenomenal success of her Harry Potter series has led to extravagant promotional campaigns, such as renting this vintage steam engine for $22,000 a day.*

1

Wild About Harry

JUST SECONDS AFTER midnight, London time, on Friday, July 7, 2000, a 12-year-old boy named Louis Shulz purchased the first copy of *Harry Potter and the Goblet of Fire*, J.K. Rowling's fourth book in the Harry Potter series. At the six-story Waterstone's bookstore in the city's Picadilly neighborhood, a line of 500 adults and children waited behind him. Many of them clutched sleeping bags for an all-night celebration hosted by the store. On the other side of the Atlantic Ocean, as Friday evening drifted toward midnight in the United States, bookstore owners and staff peeked excitedly out the windows of their stores as the crowds of Potter fans grew larger.

"I have never seen anything like this," Richard Klein, co-owner of Book Revue in Huntington, New York, had remarked earlier in the week in a *New York Times* article headlined "Harry Potter Book Becoming a Publishing Phenomenon." He said, "People are frenzied out there about this book."[1] "The anticipation is beyond anything we imagined," agreed Michael Jacobs, a senior vice president at Scholastic, Rowling's American publisher. "The book has crossed over and is now being read by adults . . . as well as children. The anticipation has allowed us to have the biggest first printing in the history of trade publishing."[2]

As the minutes ticked away, FedEx workers across the country loaded 9,000 trucks with 250,000 copies of *Harry Potter and the Goblet of Fire*, which were preordered through Amazon.com and destined to arrive on Saturday. At Point O'Pines Camp in Brant Lake, New York, a staff member asked the 300 girls at dinnertime how many expected to received a copy of Rowling's new book in the mail. About a third raised their hands.

Most of the 3.8 million copies were already stacked in bookstores, safeguarded by owners who had signed a legally binding pledge to Scholastic not to sell any copies before the midnight kickoff. "If we hear of any substantiated case of selling the books early, that bookseller will receive no subsequent shipments of Harry Potter books," said Scholastic's Jacobs. "I think everyone realizes that the stakes are high."[3] Another 2 million copies were slated for printing later in the month.

Outside the Barnes & Noble bookstore on the Upper West Side of Manhattan, 350 people—many who had waited since 10 P.M.—tugged their jackets and sweaters tighter in the unseasonably cool air. Inside the store, staffers adjusted their wizard costumes and checked the dry ice that smoked silently in cauldrons beneath the plastic spiders and star-shaped balloons that hung from the ceiling. Near the cash registers, six-foot pyramids of books, each one an earlier title in the Potter series, stood ready to be rapidly dismantled. Eighteen million copies had already been sold in Britain and the United States since the appearance of the first book, *Harry Potter and the Sorcerer's Stone*, in 1998. Behind the counter lay all the copies of the coveted fourth book.

At the Borders bookstore in Santa Fe, New Mexico, a trio of jugglers arrived to entertain the waiting crowd. A thousand miles north at Tattered Cover in Denver, the staff blended a batch of ginger ale, apple cider, and dry ice to imitate Harry's favorite drink, butterbeer.

Midnight drew near. At Books of Wonder in Manhattan, annoyed adults told the many camera crews to back off and stop pushing the kids.

At the stroke of 12:00 A.M., the news ticker in Times Square announced that *Harry Potter and the Goblet of Fire* was available in bookstores. Susan Scioli, owner of Community Bookstore in Brooklyn, drew back a curtain that covered the storefront, snapped open the lock on the front door, and watched as a witch ran out and merrily rang a gong. By 12:15 A.M., Scioli had sold out her entire allotment of 580 copies of the book—500 of which had been preordered and reserved by the customer's last name.

In Britain, the sun was just coming up. The Hogwarts Express, which carried 34-year-old J.K. Rowling, prepared to pull away from special platform nine and three-quarters in King's Cross station, London, the same spot from which Harry Potter had embarked to find his destiny at the Hogwarts School of Witchcraft and Wizardry. The vintage steam train, the oldest in Britain, had once been used by

A Harry Potter fan wearing the trademark glasses begins reading immediately at a midnight sale of Harry Potter and the Goblet of Fire *as Barnes and Noble employees, also dressed for the occasion, look on.*

royalty. Now Rowling's British publisher, Bloomsbury, was renting it for $22,000 a day to bear the reigning queen of children's writers on a four-day promotional tour through England to Perth, Scotland.

In the dining car, white linen and crystal covered the tables. Rowling told reporters that she did not feel like a celebrity, drawing smiles of disbelief. She was there for the children, she said, and she wished she could spend more time with them, instead of with reporters. Time was short, and Rowling leaned out of one of the passenger car windows and posed for a final picture. As the train left the station, crowds of adults and children who had come to see her off waved goodbye. In a sense, the colorful scene was not only about the publication of the latest Potter book, but it was also a celebration of children reading. Harry Potter had made reading cool. Children all over the world had already read the first three books and were eager for the next installment.

Rowling's first book, *Harry Potter and the Sorcerer's Stone*, was on the *New York Times* bestseller list for 14 weeks. The only other children's title to come close to that mark was E.B. White's *Charlotte's Web*, which was on the list for 3 weeks in 1952. The ripple created by Harry's popularity reached other children's books almost immediately. All seven titles of C.S. Lewis's *Chronicles of Narnia* series, originally published in 1950, doubled in sales in 2000. Sales of Lloyd Alexander's *Chronicles of Prydian* series about Taran, an assistant pig keeper, tripled. Brian Jacques's *Redwall* books spiked suddenly, as well.

Booksellers and librarians took note. Recognizing the hunger of Potter-starved readers who awaited the fourth Rowling book, Joseph-Beth Booksellers in Cincinnati started a Harry Potter Withdrawal Club, regaling its members with readings from L. Frank Baum's *The Wizard of Oz* and from Lloyd Alexander's *The Book of Three*, the first title in the *Chronicles of Prydian* series. In public libraries nationwide, Alexander's lists assuring young readers: "If you like Harry Potter, you'll like these, too. . . ." found their way into eager hands.

''I've been doing kids' books for 10 years, and I've never seen anything like this, kids coming in and saying give me something like this book," said Wendi Gratz, a children's buyer for the Joseph-Beth chain, who counted 20 children ages 9 to 13 at the inaugural meeting of the club, one of

Did you know...

Rowling dreamed about Harry Potter for the first time when she was working on the seventh book. On her Web site, on December 19, 2006, she posted this dream:

For years now, people have asked me whether I ever dream that I am "in" Harry's world. The answer was "no" until a few nights ago, when I had an epic dream in which I was, simultaneously, Harry and the narrator. I was searching for a Horcrux in a gigantic, crowded hall, which bore no resemblance to the Great Hall as I imagine it. As the narrator I knew perfectly well that the Horcrux was jammed in a hidden nook in the fireplace, while as Harry I was searching for it in all kinds of other places, while trying to make the people around me say lines I had pre-arranged for them. Meanwhile waiters and waitresses who work in the real café in which I have written huge parts of book seven roamed around me as though on stilts, all of them at least fifteen feet high. Perhaps I should cut back on the caffeine?*

*J.K. Rowling Official Site, http://www.jkrowling.com.

literally hundreds that have been organized by bookstores around the country.[4]

Now, at last, the fourth book was in the bookstores and soon to be in the children's hands. On Saturday morning, July 8, planes flying above beaches in Los Angeles, Chicago, New York, New Jersey, and Hilton Head, North Carolina towed banners in the summer sky proclaiming, "'Harry Potter and the Goblet of Fire.' Read it Now!" Over the weekend, Barnes & Noble bookstores sold a half million copies; Borders bookstores sold 200,000 copies; and Amazon.com delivered 250,000 pre-ordered copies by Saturday. Amazon.co.uk., the British subsidiary of Amazon.com, the online bookseller, said advance orders of 400,000 copies of *Harry Potter and the Goblet of Fire* made it the biggest seller in its brief history of online bookselling. Random House/Listening Library released 200,000 cassettes and CDs of Jim Dale reading *Harry Potter IV,* the largest printing to date of an audiobook children's title.

As the Hogwarts Express clanked noisily into stations, youngsters who clutched vouchers from British booksellers climbed aboard to meet Rowling. Newspapers claimed she was third among Britain's top-earning women, and Queen Elizabeth had recently elevated her to an Officer of the British Empire.

The publicity behind the sale of the fourth Harry Potter book was like nothing ever before; no book or author had experienced such fanfare. The celebration and anticipation would not stop there: Rowling still had three books to write in the series. Would each book continue to draw in fans for midnight sales and long lines? The answer would be a resounding yes.

Rowling's fifth book, *Harry Potter and the Order of the Phoenix,* delighted young people across the world. It sold an estimated 5 million copies on the first day of publication, which set sales records at bookstores throughout the United States, Canada, and the United Kingdom.

Just as before, kids waited eagerly in long lines for the fifth book, which ran a whopping 870 pages. In suburban Pittsburgh, nearly 1,000 people showed up at the Cranberry Barnes & Noble Friday night for Harry Potter fun, and the store sold over 750 copies. J.K. Rowling herself attended a midnight launch of her book in Edinburgh. "When *Goblet of Fire* was published I was desperate to go into a bookshop at midnight and see children's reactions, so this time I'm really pleased I could," she said.[5]

At Books of Wonder in New York City, about 1,000 fans, young and old, waited in line for their copies of the book. There were kids dressed in Harry Potter glasses, magical hats, and robes. First in line was 12-year-old Alexandra Korves of New York City. Her father, Douglas Korves, had saved her a spot on line at 6:30 P.M. until Alexandra joined him two hours later. They had done this before, when Alexandra was first in line to buy *Harry Potter and the Goblet of Fire* at the same store.[6]

Then, the sixth book, *Harry Potter and the Half-Blood Prince*, arrived in 2005, finding the same sort of success and popularity. In 24 hours, it sold 6.9 million copies in the United States alone, making it one of the fastest selling books ever. It generated over $100 million in sales on its opening weekend, which is more than the combined earnings of the top movies at the box office that weekend.

Now fans were just one book away from the end of the series. Anticipation for the seventh book continued to build. On December 21, 2006, a Christmas-themed hangman puzzle appeared on J.K. Rowling: The Official Web Site, www.jkrowling.com, which revealed the book's title: *Harry Potter and the Deathly Hallows*. The book was released during the summer of 2007.

By now, most of Rowling's fans know that she lives in Scotland, and that *Harry Potter and the Sorcerer's Stone* was her first published book. Rowling certainly never expected this kind of popularity and success. What is she like, this dedicated writer in whose imagination Harry Potter had suddenly appeared 10 years earlier, as she was looking out the window during a train ride to King's Cross station?

J.K. Rowling poses at the Glamour magazine Women of the Year Awards in New York City. Describing herself as a "plain young girl" when she was growing up, Rowling is now a reluctant celebrity and often seems uncomfortable being in the public spotlight.

2

"Quiet, Freckly, Short-Sighted"

J.K. ROWLING'S STORY begins, like that of her famous character, Harry Potter, at King's Cross railway station in London, where her parents met in the early 1960s. There, in one of England's largest terminals, built of iron and glass at the height of steam-powered trains in the mid nineteenth century, Peter Rowling, 19, an automotive engineer for Rolls Royce, saw a young passenger who caught his eye. Her name was Anne, and she was also 19. She was a lab technician of French and Scottish ancestry. After a courtship that lasted a year, Peter proposed to her—on another train!

Their first daughter, Joanne (J.K.) Rowling was born on July 31, 1965, near the city of Bristol at Chipping Sodbury General Hospital, "which I think is appropriate for someone who collects funny names," she commented later in a short autobiographic sketch titled "The Not Especially Fascinating Life of J.K. Rowling."[1] A second daughter, Di, was born two years later. Rowling says that the day of her sister's birth is her earliest memory. Di and Joanne were the best of friends, but like most siblings, they had their share of fights. The family lived in Yate, a small village to the west of Chipping Sodbury.

The Rowlings were affectionate parents. When Jo, as family and friends nicknamed Joanne, came down with measles at age four, her father read to her from Kenneth Grahame's *Wind in the Willows*. This book, about a series of humorous adventures involving small animals, begins, "The Mole had been working very hard all the morning, spring-cleaning his little home. First with brooms, then with dusters; then on ladders and steps and chairs, with a brush and a pail of whitewash; till he had dust in his throat and eyes, and splashes of whitewash all over his black fur, and an aching back and weary arms."[2]

Most kids like stories about animals. Just scan the children's section in a bookstore and notice how many of the stories focus on animals. As a young girl, Jo was no exception. She loved the characters in the *Wind in the Willows*, and she started telling her own stories about animals. Jo invented a story in which her sister Di fell down a rabbit-hole and lived on strawberries provided by the rabbit family. Then at age five or six, she wrote a story about a rabbit with the measles whose friends come by for visits, including a giant Miss Bee. "Rabbits loomed large in our early story-telling sessions; we badly wanted a rabbit," Rowling said. "And ever since Rabbit and Miss Bee, I have wanted to be a writer, though I rarely told anyone so. I was afraid they'd tell me I didn't have a hope."[3] Jo often entertained her sister Di with fun and adventurous stories. Sometimes the stories turned into games, in which they would "play" characters.

About that time, the family moved to the village of Winterbourne on the other side of Bristol. Jo and Di made friends with a brother and sister named Ian and Vicki Potter, who lived in the neighborhood. Jo liked the sound of "Potter" (her name is pronounced like "bowling," which inspired jokes at school about Jo "Rolling Pins"). Ian Potter led the girls in hijinks that the straitlaced Jo found thrilling. He put garden slugs on picnic plates, booby-trapped the training wheels on Vicki's bike, and dared the girls to run through wet cement, which they did. Jo liked school in Winterbourne, where she made pottery, drew, and wrote stories.

When Jo was eight, her mother gave her a book that had been one of Mrs. Rowling's favorites as a child: Elizabeth Goudge's *The Little White Horse*. Goudge, who in some ways mirrored what Rowling would become, was an outstanding writer of children's stories that often included magic spells, magic gates, long-lost relatives, and dazzling coincidences. Moreover, Goudge's writing was vivid and filled with strong visual images that conjured up a real world.

Goudge's *The Little White Horse*, set in 1842, tells the story of 13-year-old Maria Merryweather, whose father's debts have caused the family to lose the London home she loved so much. Now there is only enough money to send Maria, her dog Wiggins, and her governess, Miss Heliotrope, to live with a mysterious, distant cousin, Sir Benjamin, at Moonacre Manor. Maria unravels the secrets behind her new home by solving a series of mysteries. Rowling liked the heroine because "She was freckly, and had reddish hair. And I identified with her a lot."[4]

Of all the books Rowling read as a child, *The Little White Horse* remained her favorite. Also on her personal list of much-loved books were *I Capture the Castle* by Dodie Smith; *Manxmouse* by Paul Gallico; *A Girl of the Limberlost* by Gene Stratton-Porter; *Ballet Shoes* by Noel Streatfeild;

Did you know...

If you like the Harry Potter books, here are some other titles you may enjoy:

The Chronicles of Prydain (series) by Lloyd Alexander
The Lost Years of Merlin by T.A. Baron
The Dark Secret of Weatherend by John Bellairs
The Witches by Roald Dahl
So You Want to Be a Wizard by Diane Duane
The Neverending Story by Michael Ende
Redwall by Brian Jacques
The Dark Lord of Derkholm by Diana Wynne Jones
The Phantom Tollbooth by Norton Juster
A Wizard of Earthsea by Ursula K. Le Guin
A Wrinkle in Time by Madeline L'Engle
Five Children and It by E. Nesbit
The Golden Compass by Philip Pullman
The Hobbit by J.R.R. Tolkien
The Sword in the Stone by T.H. White
A Series of Unfortunate Events (series) by Lemony Snicket
The Chronicles of Narnia (series) by C.S. Lewis
Artemis Fowl by Eoin Colfer

Kenneth Grahame's *Wind in the Willows*; and C.S. Lewis's *The Chronicles of Narnia*. She also loved E. Nesbit, the English woman who wrote many children's books during the late nineteenth and early twentieth century, including *The Story of the Treasure Seekers* and *The Wouldbegoods.*

In 1974, when Jo was nine, the Rowlings moved about 40 miles from Winterbourne to the tiny village of Tutshill, in the Wye River valley near England's border with Wales. Rowling's parents had been raised in London, and it was one of their dreams to live in the country.

The Wye valley, a little more than 100 miles from London, is a remarkably beautiful part of England. The poet William Wordsworth, who vacationed near the river in the summer of 1798, was moved to write about "These waters, rolling from their mountain-springs/With soft inland murmur," and "steep and lofty cliffs" that "connect/ The landscape with the quiet of the sky." Within 20 miles of Tutshill are Tintern Abbey—one of the most romantic-looking ruins in Britain, Chepstow Castle, and Raglan Castle, which are all likely to impress a child with imagination. Rowling recalls that she and her sister were allowed to roam the banks of the Wye and explore the southern-most part of the Royal Forest of Dean, which covers the valley like a green scarf.

The Forest of Dean is centuries old and was originally set aside for royal hunting. Later, timber from the forest was used to fuel iron furnaces during the Industrial Revolution and to supply the British navy with masts, yardarms, and planks. In 1938, the government designated it a National Forest Park, the first in England. Parts of the forest are quite remote, accessible only by lonely roads and footpaths. Perhaps Rowling was thinking of the Forest of Dean when she described the Forbidden Forest in *Harry Potter and the Sorcerer's Stone:* "[Hagrid] led them to the very edge of the forest. Holding his lamp up high, he pointed down a narrow, winding earth track that disappeared into the thick black trees. A light breeze lifted their hair as they looked into the forest."[5]

School, on the other hand, was a disappointment. On her first morning at Tutshill Primary, Jo failed a test on fractions. The teacher, she said, had the pupils divided into "smart" rows on the left and "stupid" rows on the right. As the new girl who could not do fractions, Jo ended up on the right side. Eventually, the teacher ordered Jo to swap seats with her best friend in a left-hand row, which hurt their friendship.

Rowling described herself as "quiet, freckly, short-sighted child."[6] She wore very thick eyeglasses, which she received for free from the National Health Service. This, she has said, is why Harry wears glasses. She was a bookish and smart child and she could be both shy and bossy.

From this contradictory mixture of traits, she later created Hermione Granger, perhaps her second most memorable character after Harry Potter. From the instant Hermione marches into the train compartment where Harry and Ron Weasley are sitting, Rowling paints a portrait of a take-charge girl: "'Has anyone see a toad? Neville's lost one,' she said. She had a bossy sort of voice, lots of bushy brown hair, and rather large front teeth." Rowling has said that Hermione is based partially on herself at 11. "I did not set out to make Hermione like me but she is a bit like me. She is an exaggeration of how I was when I was younger."[7] Rowling does not think she was quite such a know-it-all, but she was very committed to academic achievement. Her bossiness was probably to compensate for her shyness and insecurity.

Short and squat, Rowling was no athlete. In the Harry Potter books, she chose to make the sport Quidditch important at Hogwarts because "sport is such an important part of life at school. I am terrible at all sports, but I gave my hero a talent I'd love to have had. Who wouldn't want to fly?"[8]

Although Rowling takes some details from her own life, she could not rely on her own school experiences to create Hogwarts, a setting that tests the cleverness and stamina of her characters. Rowling did not attend boarding school, and she had no desire whatsoever to go to one. She told Stephen Fry, who is the voice for the Harry Potter audiobooks sold in the United Kingdom, that she had never even been inside a boarding school, but that she knew from the start that this was where Harry must go. She commented:

> But it was essential for the plot that the children could be enclosed somewhere together overnight. This could not be a day school, because the adventure would fall down . . . every second day if they went home and spoke to their parents. . . . This is a place where there are going to be lots of noises, smells, flashing lights. And you would want to contain it somewhere fairly distant so that Muggles didn't come across it all the time.[9]

Rowling's parents enrolled her at a day school called Wyedean Comprehensive at about the same age that Harry started at Hogwarts. She must have felt a little apprehensive, having heard the same rumor about Wyedean that Dudley tells Harry about Stonewall High: that older children put the new students' heads in the toilet. It turned out to be a traditional myth meant to make new students nervous, and Rowling soon settled in. During lunch, she entertained friends with long stories that unfolded every day, in which

Jessica Mitford was an English journalist. As a teenager, J.K. Rowling greatly admired Mitford's socialist beliefs, independent lifestyle, and inner strength.

each of them faced some incredible challenge and won; this was later a key story element in all of her books.

One of Rowling's listeners and most devoted friends was a classmate named Sean Harris, who became the model for Ron Weasley. On her Web site, Rowling recalled, "He was the first of my friends to learn to drive and that turquoise and white car meant FREEDOM . . . some of the happiest memories of my teenage years involve zooming off into the darkness in Sean's car."[10] Sean was the first person with whom Rowling discussed her ambition to become a writer, and "he was also the only person who thought I was bound to be a success at it."[11]

When Rowling was a young teenager, she found a hero whose strength, independence, and opinions she could admire: an English journalist named Jessica Mitford. As teenagers, both Joanne and Di were attracted to social causes. When Rowling was 14, her aunt told her that social activist Jessica Mitford had bought a camera that she charged to her father and then went traveling. Jessica Mitford had been born into wealth, but she came to believe that socialism—shared ownership of factories, mines, railroads, and land—would create a more just society, a view that offended her family. Traveling to Spain in the late 1930s to fight on the side of the Communists in the Spanish Civil War, Mitford met and married a soldier who was later killed in World War II. In the 1950s, she broke away from the Communist Party when she decided that she could no longer support the policies of the Soviet Union. Instead, she put her energies into becoming a muckraking journalist, someone who investigates corruption and injustice. Her best-known book, *An American Way of Death* (1963), attacked the funeral industry for permitting greedy and deceptive practices.

Rowling admired Mitford for her political views and especially for her determination to carry on after the deaths of three of her children. Later, Rowling named her daughter after her hero, explaining, "I found her inspiring because she was a brave and idealistic person—the qualities I most admire, in other words."[12] In *Harry Potter and the Goblet of Fire*, Rowling paid tribute to Mitford when Hermione defied authority and championed the rights of elves.

It was fortunate that, at this point in her life, Rowling found a hero who was able to continue after terrible personal loss. That same year, in 1980, Rowling's mother, Anne, was diagnosed with multiple sclerosis.

J.K. Rowling was photographed at a press conference in Toronto. Although she is occasionally annoyed by the perception that she was penniless before finding success with her writing, the truth is that she did struggle through dull occupations whose only saving grace was the free time they allowed her to work on her books.

3

Harry Appears

ANNE ROWLING WAS 35 when she was diagnosed with multiple sclerosis, a disorder of the central nervous system. Rowling was 15 when she learned of her mother's condition. The news must have hit her hard. Many years later, Rowling wrote on her Web site, "I think most people believe, deep down, that their mothers are indestructible; it was a terrible shock to hear that she had an incurable illness, but even then, I did not fully realise what the diagnosis might mean."[1]

As a way to cope, Rowling created two identities: one to please her family, and one to please herself. On the one hand, she became head girl, or first in her class, at Wyedean Comprehensive, despite her later statements that she was a terrible student. Along with the honor came duties she did not enjoy very much, but she accepted them. Once, she had to escort "Lady Somebody" around the school fair. Another time, she was asked to lead a school assembly. To limit her role as master of ceremonies, she played a record instead, which backfired, as the music started skipping over and over. Rowling stood there, mortified, until the Head Mistress kicked the record player.

On the other hand, Rowling discovered that adopting a more devil-may-care attitude suited her too, and it probably helped conceal her fears about her mother. Now that she wore contact lenses instead of glasses, Rowling felt more confident. She discovered that it was fun to attract disapproving looks from adults when she and some tough-looking boys in leather jackets shared cigarettes at the bus stop every morning. She thought her idol, Jessica Mitford, the social activist who did things her way, would approve.

Despite this rebellion, Rowling was a good student. After she was graduated from Wyedean, she enrolled at the University of Exeter in the southwest corner of England, a selective school of 10,000 students with several campuses.

Rowling's humanities classes met at the Streatham campus, the largest and busiest of the university's three sites, set on 245 hilly acres. A Web site that welcomes new students to Exeter boasts that the campus is "readily acknowledged as one of the most beautiful in the country. . . . its lakes, parkland, woodland and gardens make it a very special place that offers a safe and enjoyable environment for study."[2] Again, Rowling had high grades. Her only academic shortcomings were that she checked out library books and failed to return them on time. Once, she ran up late fines that totaled more than the equivalent of $250. After she paid the charges, she did the same thing again.

In college, students must choose a major, and Rowling later confessed that she chose the wrong one. Her parents persuaded her to study French as a steppingstone to a career in international business. Her first love in school had always been English, although she had never confided her hopes of being a writer to any of her teachers. When Rowling had to pursue a field of study for a degree, she ignored her instincts and opted for French and Classics. She later advised some Harry Potter fans who interviewed her not to follow her example, but to listen to their own hearts when it was time to make career choices. "So learn from my mistake—do what you want, not what your parents want!"[3] Nevertheless, as part of her studies, she dutifully went to Paris for a year to work as a teaching assistant. In 1987, she graduated from Exeter. At the ceremony, her mother watched from a wheelchair in the audience, noticeably worse in health than she had been six years before.

As a new graduate, the young French major started to look for jobs and moved to London. She still hoped to become a writer, and so she sought a position where the work would be a good fit with her secret ambition. She accepted a job as a researcher and bilingual secretary with Amnesty International, an organization that champions the rights of political prisoners and campaigns against human rights abuses all over the world. Rowling found that, in an office of thinkers and readers like herself, she could sneak time at her desk for creative writing now and then. During meetings, she doodled odd names such as "Dumbledore," a medieval word for bumblebee, and she imagined what a character with such a name would be like.

It became clear to Rowling that she was just killing time with office work. She needed to change jobs, and she found a position as a secretary in Manchester this time. This job was routine and mainly involved filing and typing, which she found tedious. Rowling also felt too disorganized to be a good secretary. Outside of work, she wrote for long hours, preferring to sit at a quiet table in a pub or café. She eventually completed one novel for adults and half of another, but she was not satisfied with either effort.

One day during a train ride from Manchester to London in 1990, she got an idea for a long, rich story that captivated her. The train trip should have been a short hop between cities, with a final stop at King's Cross station, but delays prolonged the journey. Rowling felt bored, and she stared out the train window at cows in a pasture. Suddenly, for no reason she can recall, Harry Potter appeared in her mind.

It was an incredible feeling to suddenly have so much of this idea come to her at once. She explained, "I had been writing almost continuously since the age of six but I had never been so excited about an idea before."[4] The character she envisioned, "this scrawny, black-haired bespectacled boy" to whom unexplainable things kept happening, did not know his own power.[5] Rowling knew that the boy was a wizard, but he did not know he was a wizard. He became more and more real to her, and her mind spun with ideas about him. Rowling thought she should write them down. Then, to "my immense frustration, I didn't have a functioning pen with me, and I was

Daniel Radcliffe, the star of the Harry Potter movies, poses just prior to beginning work on the first movie. To many readers, Radcliffe is exactly the "scrawny, black-haired bespectacled boy" Rowling imagined.

too shy to ask anybody if I could borrow one. I think, now, that this frustration was probably a good thing, because I simply sat and thought."[6]

The day-dreamed story enthralled her. Like a game, the tale could have hidden clues, formulas for spells, and humorous and threatening characters. So much could take place during the education of a young wizard that more than

Did you know...

An author rarely comes up with a completely original idea. Other authors have explored settings and characters similar to Rowling's. What matters is how a story develops, how well it is told, and what themes are explored. For example:

- *The Worst Witch* (1974) series by Jill Murphy for young readers (7–11 years old) is about Mildred, a student at Miss Cackle's Academy for Witches, who does everything wrong.

- *Witch Week* (1982) by Diana Wynne Jones is a darkly funny suspense story about an outbreak of illegal magic in school full of witch orphans whose parents have been burned as witches.

- *The Books of Magic* (1990) by Neil Gaiman features a dark-haired, bespectacled boy who discovers he is a wizard. A magic owl accompanies him.

- Rowling has said that Harry Potter has a "spiritual ancestor": Wart, the young King Arthur in T.H. White's *The Once and Future King*.

one book would be needed to tell everything from beginning to end.

For the next four hours as the train ambled toward King's Cross, Rowling let her imagination play with the problem of how Harry Potter would become a wizard. First, something would have to distinguish him as exceptional, and a lightening-shaped scar seemed right. Then he would be summoned to attend a boarding school for wizardry. A boarding school would be best because the characters would stay there at night, a perfect setting for magical events. The school building would be rather dreary and have ghosts, too. As she thought about ghosts, the characters Nearly Headless Nick and Peeves seemed to appear to her fully sketched out. Another advantage of a boarding school would be that all the wizards-in-training would be among peers for months, free from interfering grownups, except for their instructors in magic. Finally, the location of this school would be a mystery. Hidden from ordinary people, it would be in plain sight only to the select few who could enter through its enchanted doors.

At last, the train arrived in King's Cross station, where platform nine and three-quarters would one day become as famous as the wardrobe in C.S. Lewis's *The Chronicles of Narnia*. Rowling was ready to write about the secret of Harry Potter and his world. As she returned to Manchester, she hoped that none of her officemates would invite her to lunch. She wanted to spend time by herself in pubs and cafés so she could sketch out this story that absorbed her. Over the next five years, she outlined the plots for each book and began to write the first novel.

Rowling could not have started these books without the clear vision of Harry Potter, glasses and all. She has said that of all the characters, she most strongly identifies with Harry. "I have to think myself into his head far more than any of the others, because everything is seen from his point of view. But there's a little bit of me in most of the characters."[7]

This helped to relieve the tedium of Rowling's office job a little, but her inspiration for Harry Potter may have come at a good time in her life for another reason. Her mother's illness was quite advanced. Rowling tried to remain defiantly optimistic, denying that the end was near. In retrospect, though, she realized that her mother had gotten worse. Her mobility was limited, and she looked very ill and exhausted.

On December 30, 1990, Rowling's father went upstairs for a routine check on his wife. After battling multiple sclerosis for 10 years, Anne Rowling had finally succumbed. She had died at age 45 of respiratory failure. Rowling said her mother's death "changed both my world and Harry's forever."[8]

Rowling was unprepared. Despite the grim disease and her mother's worsening health, she had believed that her mother would be around for many more years. She just could not accept that her mother was gone. It was a terrible time. Rowling recalled, "My father, Di and I were devastated; she was only forty-five years old and we had never imagined—probably because we could not bear to contemplate the idea—that she could die so young. I remember feeling as though there was a paving slab pressing down upon my chest, a literal pain in my heart."[9] Over 20 years later, Rowling would say, "Barely a day goes by when I do not think of her. There would be so much to tell her, impossibly much."[10]

The loss of her mother would be the most difficult thing that Rowling had ever faced, but she would work through her grief by writing the first Harry Potter book in earnest in another country—Portugal.

Rowling ended up living in the quays of Oporto, Portugal (above), after her mother died. There she began work on the book that would become Harry Potter and the Sorcerer's Stone. *While in Portugal, Rowling was briefly married to journalist Jorge Arantes, with whom she had a daughter, Jessica.*

4

Half a Suitcase of Stories

NINE MONTHS AFTER her mother's death, Rowling accepted a position abroad to teach English as a foreign language. She needed to get away: She felt shattered by her mother's death, and wanted to start over in a new place. She explained, "A lot of bad stuff had happened, and I needed to sort myself out a bit."[1]

Rowling went to Oporto, Portugal, a center of European trade since the twelfth century. Oporto sits on a sunny terraced slope that rises from the Duoro River on Portugal's northern coast. Steeped in history from the days of the Portuguese Empire, rich in architecture by the Romans, Moors, and

Christian Crusaders, the tangled medieval side streets must have offered Rowling a welcome change in scenery.

When Rowling's students gently teased their 26-year-old teacher about her last name, calling her Miss "Rolling Stone," she laughed. She liked to teach English to beginners, and her hours were perfect, too; she worked afternoons and evenings, which left her mornings open to write.

Even though the broad outline of her brewing story had occurred to Rowling on the train from Manchester to London, it would take two years to develop the intricacies of the plot. Progress was glacially slow on the first book, *Harry Potter and the Philosopher's Stone* (titled *Harry Potter and the Sorcerer's Stone* in the United States). She started the first chapter 10 different ways, and she always wrote in longhand, her preference for early drafts.

Journalists have suggested to Rowling that she immersed herself in Harry Potter to escape from her grief over her mother's death. Rowling takes offense at this, and she points out that the inspiration for the story and the preliminary work began six months earlier. Rowling also realized, "I was writing Harry Potter at the moment my mother died. I had never told her about Harry Potter."[2]

A hint of contradiction creeps in, however, when Rowling admits that dealing with loss is a part of writing and reading. Drawing on her own feelings of loss, in fact, Rowling produced one of the most memorable scenes in *Harry Potter and the Philosopher's Stone* in Chapter 12, "The Mirror of Erised." After her mother died, she was able to deepen Harry's feelings about his own dead parents. In her first few weeks in Portugal, she wrote this chapter, in which Harry sees his long-dead parents in a magic mirror:

> He looked in the mirror again. A woman standing right behind his reflection was smiling at him and waving. He reached out

a hand and felt the air behind him. If she was really there, he'd touch her, their reflections were so close together, but he felt only air—she and the others existed only in the mirror. . . . The Potters smiled and waved at Harry and he stared hungrily back at them, his hands pressed flat against the glass as though he was hoping to fall right through it and reach them. He had a powerful kind of ache inside him, half joy, half terrible sadness.

"The mirror is almost painfully from my own feelings about my mother's death," Rowling admitted to a reporter for *The Guardian* newspaper in Manchester, England.[3] "Erised," as Harry learns, is "desire" spelled backwards; when Harry looks in the mirror, he sees what he most wants to see. She added that, if she were looking in the mirror, she would see exactly what Harry saw. "I'd gabble on and at the end of five minutes I'd realize I hadn't asked what it's like to be dead. It's the selfishness of the child, isn't it?—at least I'm aware of that. But it couldn't be long enough."[4]

After her mother's death, Rowling did not permit herself the needed time to grieve. Her attitude was "Let's keep going and keep moving." Hence, she picked up and moved far away, which led her on a bumpy path. Barely a year after she arrived in Portugal, Rowling married journalist Jorge Arantes on October 16, 1992. In 1993, her daughter Jessica was born, whom she named for Jessica Mitford, Rowling's real-life heroine. Not long after, however, the marriage disintegrated for reasons known only to Rowling and Arantes. Rowling usually changes the subject when an interviewer mentions her brief first marriage. Although the marriage did not last, the birth of her first daughter was one of the best things in her life. Rowling left Portugal, taking Jessica with her.

Rowling visited her sister in Edinburgh, Scotland (above), and decided that it would be a good city to settle in while she finished her novel and worked as a French teacher.

Suddenly Rowling, a single parent and temporarily job-less, was on her own. At Christmas, she went to Edinburgh, Scotland, to stay a few weeks with her sister, Di. Her plan was to stay only long enough to figure out what to do next, but the city began to charm her. Edinburgh, Scotland's capital city, looks like a theater backdrop to an eighteenth-century play. Church spires poke out everywhere above the gray-brown stone buildings of the skyline. Steeply-built streets roll up and down green hillsides and meander through parks. Perched high above the city, atop a rocky crag, sits Edinburgh Castle, sections of which are 900 years old. Strictly on a practical level, Rowling considered the free museums, the manageable size of the city, and the good public transportation. She thought she could give her daughter a better life here while she lived on a low-income budget.

When Rowling had left Portugal, half her suitcase was stuffed with papers covered with stories about Harry Potter. Now that she had found a good place to settle down with Jessica, she vowed to finish the novel before she started to work as a French teacher, and to try to get it published.

As usual, Rowling forced herself to be optimistic, even though her circumstances were hardly ideal for an unpub-lished writer. Mice would run out from under the furniture and scratch at the walls at night in the tiny, chilly apart-ment she rented. It was against the policy of public daycare centers to take babies, and no full-time job paid enough to make private daycare affordable. For 18 months, Rowling relied on welfare payments, as she supplemented the money with income from part-time work. She felt lonely and frus-trated, but she was determined to meet her self-imposed deadline to finish her novel. As she wheeled her daughter in a stroller through the streets of Edinburgh, she would stop somewhere for tea and write a little if Jessica fell asleep. A favorite haunt was Nicholson's Café because it was quiet. She also wrote at the Elephant House Café. Rowling wrote nearly every evening.

Thoughts that she was letting her daughter down sometimes assailed Rowling. A particularly bad moment came when she visited another mother with a baby boy about her daughter's age and saw the little boy's bedroom full

Did you know...

Jim Dale, the British-born actor who lives in New York, has narrated all of the Listening Library audiobooks from the Harry Potter series in the United States. He had never recorded an audiobook before he worked on Harry Potter. Dale began in the entertainment business as a comedian, and he has also been a disc jockey and a pop singer. He then became an actor, and has appeared on the stage, in films, and on television. Although many might not be familiar with his face, his voice is recognizable to most fans. Dale typically reads chronological chunks of the book to himself silently at night, then records the next day in a studio. He reads about 20 double-spaced manuscript pages an hour, and he stops when he senses that his voice is tiring. According to Dale, who has created more than 200 character voices, it is not so difficult to keep all the voices straight. The hardest part is to sit absolutely still, because the microphones can pick up the rustle of cloth from his pants as he crosses his legs.

Rowling lived in a tiny, underheated apartment in Edinburgh while she was writing the first Harry Potter book, so she did much of her work in cafes like the Elephant House, pictured above.

of toys. By comparison, when Rowling packed her daughter's toys away, they all fit into a shoebox. For months, a fit of depression clouded her thoughts. Later, this feeling inspired the Dementors, who suck all hope and good thoughts out of their victims in *Harry Potter and the Prisoner of Azkaban*.

There have been many rumors about Rowling's financial status during the time she was writing Harry Potter. Although it is true that she lived on a very low income for much of the time, she was not utterly destitute. Once, someone asked her if she had saved the used napkins on which she had written the first manuscript. She responded, joking, "We really need to squash this myth before people ask to see the used tea bags on which I drafted the first book!"[5] Of course, the manuscript was written on notebook paper. There has also been much made of her status as a single mother. "There was a point where I really felt I had 'penniless divorcee lone parent' tattooed on my head. . . . You couldn't read about Harry Potter without seeing that somewhere in the piece."[6] Sometimes society attaches a stigma to single motherhood, but Rowling has made it clear that she never felt ashamed about being a single parent.

Eventually, after struggling financially, Rowling found a typing job that paid a good wage. She squeezed in coursework that would earn her a teaching certificate in Scotland, too. The whole time no one knew she was working on a novel except her sister, who encouraged her to keep on, and her ex-husband, who knew about her aspirations. Just once she confided the secrets of her writing life to a friend. The woman gave her an incredulous look, as though she had said she thought she could solve her problems by winning the lottery.

In 1995, Rowling finished *Harry Potter and the Philosopher's Stone*, typing the manuscript on an old second-hand typewriter. All this time, she had not made any contacts in the publishing world or enlisted any agents to represent her. Unable to afford the cost of duplicating her 80,000-word original typed manuscript, she spent weeks typing a backup copy for herself.

Rowling then mailed the first three sample chapters of the novel that she had worked so hard on to an agent who promptly returned it. Trying again, she chose the Christopher Little Literary Agency from a directory because she liked the sound of the name. Once more, she sent the chapters to someone she had never met, and waited. The odds of the book being published were almost as likely as winning the lottery.

Rowling signs a copy of one of her books for essay contest winners in New York. Another unique promotional campaign involved the essay contest "How the Harry Potter Books Have Changed My Life."

5

Bidding War

EVERY AGENT AND publishing house has a stack of unso-
licited manuscripts called the slush pile. Sometimes, real gems
can be found in it: well-written stories that some undiscovered
talents have submitted. More often than not, a manuscript by
an unknown writer tends to be returned, provided a return
envelope is included. Otherwise, the piece gets tossed in a
wastebasket. The editor might send a reply letter that says, in
effect, "Thanks, but no thanks."

Unknowingly, Rowling had put herself at a disadvantage
with Christopher Little from the start. There was very little

chance that he would want to be her agent, because he did not even take on children's authors as clients. Through a fluke, however, her submission landed on the top of the slush pile. An agent pulled her thick envelope out of the pile, opened it, and read its contents.

Not long after, Rowling received a letter at her apartment in Edinburgh from the Christopher Little Literary Agency. Expecting a few sentences of rejection, she steeled herself to be disappointed; instead, the letter said, "Thank you. We would be pleased to receive the balance of your manuscript on an exclusive basis." Not only did this mean that Little was interested in her novel, but he wanted to make certain that Rowling did not show it to any of his competitors. She read the letter eight times in disbelief. Some authors get their books published without an agent, but it is quite rare. For a first-timer like Rowling, it can be an especially big advantage to have an agent who knows the publishing industry and can guide a client to the doorstep of the right publishing house. With Little's help, Rowling had good reason to be excited. Little's offer meant that he believed in her as a writer.

Still, this was just the first step. An agent's job is to market the manuscript to various publishers, who may or may not think the book is worth their time and money. Trusting her agent, Rowling waited on pins and needles.

Now that Rowling had met her goal and finished her novel, she found a position as a French teacher in a Scottish high school. In grade school, her nickname had been "rolling pins," like bowling pins. In Portugal, her students dubbed her Miss Rolling Stone. Now, she laughed when students serenaded her with the theme from the television program *Rawhide*, as they sang "Rolling, rolling, rolling . . .

keep those wagons rolling!" They also loved doing impressions of her English accent, which to their Scottish ears sounded drowsy and bored.

Although Rowling was comfortable with her students, she still kept part of her life hidden from them. She did not want anybody to know that she was an aspiring writer who hoped desperately to get published. One day, when a student announced that she had no paper to write with, Rowling gave her the usual warning and instructed her to tear a sheet out of the notebook on Rowling's desk. The girl lingered over the notebook for a minute, reading a page of her teacher's handwriting. Then she asked if she was a writer. Rowling was embarrassed and told the student that writing was just a hobby. In truth, though, it was more than that; she had always felt that she could not stop writing. In fact, she was already busy on a second Harry Potter novel: *Harry Potter and the Chamber of Secrets.*

Christopher Little was having difficulty finding takers for *Harry Potter and the Philosopher's Stone.* Major publishers turned it down, including HarperCollins and Penguin. One editor decided that a story set in a boarding school probably would not interest young readers because the setting was too strange. All the publishers who gave it thumbs down mentioned that it was too long; in book form, it would be hundreds of pages. What youngster would want to plow through a book like that when R.L. Stein's short Goosebumps titles sold millions of copies? From publishers' reactions, Rowling concluded that if her novel were ever to see the light of day, it would not sell very well. Twelve publishers rejected the novel.

Then Christopher Little tried Bloomsbury Publishing, a small firm in London. Founded barely 10 years earlier in 1986 by four entrepreneurs, Bloomsbury was on the lookout for rare finds. An editor at Bloomsbury dutifully scanned the opening page of Harry Potter and began to read on, passing chapters as they were read to colleagues around the office. The company's chairman gave the first chapter to his eight-year-old daughter, and she was hooked; she demanded more chapters.

The next day, Rowling received a call from her agent. "We've got a deal at Bloomsbury," Little told her. They were offering $3,600. Rowling joyfully accepted. For days she felt as though she were walking on air, knowing that her book was actually going to be in stores. There was a similar feeling at Bloomsbury.

One touchy issue remained to be addressed, however: How should the author's name appear on the cover? A female author might discourage boys. What about initials instead? Rowling, too happy to care about so small a detail at that point, agreed. Rowling used her own first initial, and then used K for "Kathleen," her grandmother's name. She does not have a middle name.

Next, Bloomsbury contracted with Rowling to print a mere 500 copies of *Harry Potter and the Philosopher's Stone*, which seems especially comical now. The publishers never dreamed it would become such an international hit. The editor, Barry Cunningham, even advised Rowling to get a day job. He thought there was little chance that a children's book could make a big splash. How wrong he was! Both girls and boys were immediately drawn into the magic world of Harry Potter: the humor, conflict, adventure, and fantasy.

As the book opens, the evil wizard Voldemort has tried to kill a family of wizards. He killed James and Lily Potter, but he failed to destroy the couple's one-year-old infant, Harry, who somehow deflected Voldemort's awful powers. The terrible encounter has left Harry with a lightning-shaped scar on his forehead. Friends of Harry's parents whisk away the now-legendary child to safekeeping with his Muggle (nonmagical) suburban middle-class aunt and uncle, Petunia and Vernon Dursley, and their bullying, overweight son, Dudley.

Ten years later, Harry is suffering through a lonely childhood, forced to live in the cupboard under the stairs at the home of the Dursleys. He knows nothing about his heritage or about his fame in the wizard world. The Dursleys punish Harry when he does anything unusual, such as communicating in a friendly way with a snake at the zoo.

Then, a messenger from the world of magic named Hagrid confronts the Dursleys and invites Harry to enroll at Hogwarts School of Witchcraft and Wizardry. He takes the bewildered youngster to shop for school supplies such as a cauldron and wand, and offers the first sign of affection that Harry can remember. Uncle Vernon is outraged and tries to prevent Harry from pursuing his destiny.

Despite his uncle's protests, Harry departs for Hogwarts from platform nine and three-quarters at London's King's Cross station. On the train, Harry becomes acquainted with his soon-to-be best friend, Ron Weasley. Hogwarts has four houses for students: Gryffindor, Ravenclaw, Hufflepuff, and the sinister Slytherin. First-year students are placed into the appropriate house by a singing Sorting Hat; Harry is assigned to Gryffindor. Harry's life takes an upturn when he finds he is a natural broomstick flyer. He is even picked for the Gryffindor Quidditch team. Quidditch, a high-flying game with three kinds of balls and seven players per team, is rough and can result in injuries. Madam Pomfrey, the school nurse, cures the students with special spells and the magic of rest.

Harry's first year at Hogwarts is filled with adventure, friendship, and danger. He finds the Mirror of Erised, and he mourns the loss of his parents when he sees them in the mirror's reflection. Harry realizes that he must be on guard against his own enemies too, such as Potions teacher Severus Snape and classmate Draco Malfoy. With his Gryffindor friends Ron Weasley and Hermione Granger, Harry tries to prevent the sorcerer's stone from falling into the hands of Voldemort and his allies. The stone offers eternal life and hence would be the key to Voldemort's plans to return to power.

We now know that this first book was just the beginning, but at the time, everyone expected that it would just be a single book (except for Rowling, of course). Once *Harry Potter and the Philosopher's Stone* was published, bookstore orders perked along but did not break records. Meanwhile, Rowling had won a grant from the Scottish Arts Council that enabled her to keep writing. Writing was what she loved to do, and she was happy that the grant helped her to devote more time to it. Thrilled that her book was published, Rowling had no idea that it was about to blow open the world of publishing.

Everything changed at the September 1997 Bologna Book Fair in Italy. Bloomsbury offered foreign publishing rights for one of their latest books by an unknown author named J.K. Rowling. Publishers sometimes hope to boost sales by reselling the rights to a book to publishers in other countries.

Attending the Bologna Book Fair was Arthur A. Levine, vice president of Scholastic Book Group, who was scouting the exhibition booths for fantasy titles that might do well in the United States. He picked up a complete, preprint layout of Harry Potter and read it on the plane back to New York. The engaging, fast-paced, and imaginative story delighted him, with its themes of friendship, loyalty, and courage holding the story together. Unfortunately, Levine was not alone in uncovering a winner. By the time he arrived in New York, nine other publishers were prepared to bid on rights to the book, and Bloomsbury found itself in the highly desirable position of conducting a spirited auction for a book it had purchased for only $3,600. Christopher Little phoned his client in Edinburgh and said her book was the contested prize between heavyweight publishers that included Hyperion, Putnam, Random House, and Scholastic. Rowling assumed a few thousand dollars were at stake and waited patiently for the result.

The phone ran late at night in Rowling's apartment. On the line was Arthur Levine, still at his office in New York because of the five-hour time difference. He told her that Scholastic had successfully purchased the rights from Bloomsbury to publish *Harry Potter and the Philosopher's Stone* for $105,000, a very high amount for an unknown author. "Don't be scared," he told her. She replied, "Thanks; I am."[1]

Like a spell, feelings of disbelief clung to Rowling for the next few days. She had never expected to make that kind of money. Her teaching contract had expired the previous summer, and Rowling realized that now she did not even have to substitute teach. She could be a full-time writer, as she had always dreamed.

Over the next few weeks, Levine enlisted Rowling's help to tailor her novel for the children's book market in the United States. Americans, for instance, would better understand the phrase "philosopher's stone" in the title if it were "sorcerer's stone." Likewise, three kinds of changes were necessary to make the text for suitable for Americans. The first were spelling changes: "gray" for "grey," "color" for "colour," "pajamas" for "pyjamas," and so on. The second were differences in common words or phrases: the American term "sweater" for the British "jumper," "taped" for "sellotaped," "mail" for "post," and so on. The third kind of change was to find American equivalents to English experiences, which was a little trickier. The English have crumpets for breakfast, for instance. Americans have, well, English muffins. Rowling could see the wisdom in all of this; as the plot, characters, and themes were more critical than anything else, she agreed to the modifications.

Not everyone approved of the attempt to Americanize the speech in *Harry Potter and the Sorcerer's Stone*. In an essay in the *New York Times*, "Harry Potter, Minus a Certain Flavour," Peter Gleik complained:

> Do we really want children to think that crumpets are the same as English muffins? Frankly reading about Harry and Hermione eating crumpets during tea is far more interesting to an American than reading about them eating English muffins during a meal. Are any books immune from this kind of devolution from English to "American" English? Would we sit back and let publishers rewrite Charles Dickens or Shakespeare? I can see it now: "A Christmas Song," "A Story of Two Cities," "The Salesman of Venice." By protecting our children from an occasional misunderstanding or trip to the dictionary we are pretending that other cultures are, or should be, the same as ours.[2]

However, Levine and Rowling explained that they only made changes when they thought American readers might

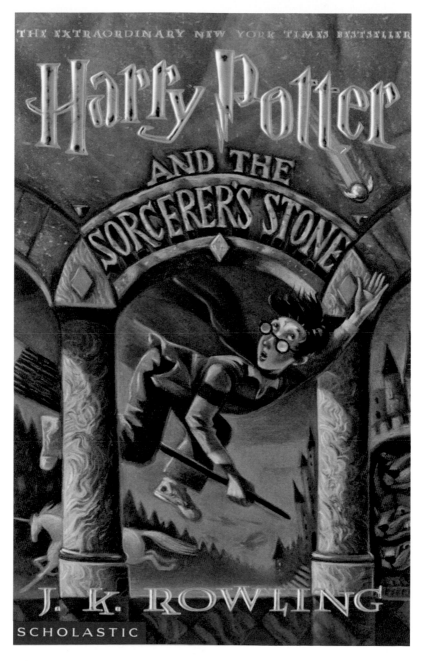

The U.S. version of Rowling's first book was called Harry Potter and the Sorcerer's Stone. *Language within the book was changed, as well, because the publishers were worried that American readers would be turned off by the British slang and references Rowling used.*

be confused, and they were careful not to lose the flavor of the language. For example, "jumper," means a dress in American English, so they translated that to "sweater," which is closer to Rowling's meaning. Although many modifications were made in the first book, each subsequent book has had fewer and fewer changes.

Then Levine began to dress up the printed book itself. The cover of the British edition, illustrated by Thomas Taylor, firmly established Harry's appearance. (Bloomsbury also printed a serious-looking cover for adults that featured a photograph of a steam train so that they could feel more comfortable about reading a children's book in public.) Levine selected Mary GrandPré to illustrate the U.S. edition and added rich paper and decorative chapter illustrations to the Scholastic edition, as well. GrandPré is known for her memorable, haunting, and dramatic work. The illustrator felt as though she already had a very strong picture of Harry in her head from the way Rowling described him. On the covers, GrandPré illustrates Harry so that he looks a little older with each book. As Harry gains confidence, his smile grows wider with each cover.

Since its debut in the United Kingdom in June 1997, sales of the novel had grown. Reviews were ecstatic, and more and more children read and loved the book. Then, in 1998, *Harry Potter and the Sorcerer's Stone* appeared in the United States. The power of Scholastic's book club, with 80 million members, helped Rowling's book effortlessly climb the bestseller lists. Two Hollywood studios expressed interest in a film version.

Media excitement on the overnight success of Harry Potter temporarily overwhelmed the young author. Worried that the next book in the series, *Harry Potter and the Chamber of Secrets,* would not be as good, Rowling struggled with a case of writer's block and the pressure of the sequel's anticipation. This was the only time, so far, that Rowling felt as though she suffered badly from writer's block. "I had my first burst of publicity about the first book

Did you know...

The Canadian version of the fifth book, *Harry Potter and the Rise of the Phoenix*, is published on 100 percent recycled paper that is chlorine-free, as well as free of fibers from ancient forests. This saved 29,640 trees in the initial print run of one million books. Before and after its release, the environmental organization Greenpeace and the National Wildlife Federation urged fans in the United States to buy the sixth book, *Harry Potter and the Half-Blood Prince*, from the book's Canadian publisher, Raincoast Books. The U.S. edition of the book, published by Scholastic Press, was printed with a percentage of recycled paper that Scholastic declined to make public. The Scholastic hardcover edition of the book claims, on the last page, to be free of fibers from ancient forests.

and it paralyzed me. I was scared the second book wouldn't measure up, but I got through it!"[3]

By now, Rowling already had the seven-book series clearly mapped out; in fact, she even had the ending to the final book written. Although Bloomsbury had not contracted with her for more than one book, she had nevertheless been working on the entire series, even as *Harry Potter and the Philosopher's Stone* made its modest debut with 500 copies. This turned out to be a fortunate decision on her part, as well as a tremendous stroke of financial luck for her publishers.

Many authors of books for children and adolescents wait years before they write a sequel, during which time their readers outgrow the stories. For example, Beverly Cleary published a new book about Ramona in 1999. The first Ramona book was published in 1952, and until 1999, the most recent was from 1984. Rowling, however, kept most of her readers interested because she was ready with a second title in the series. No sooner had *Harry Potter and the Sorcerer's Stone* achieved bestseller status in the United States than word circulated among Rowling fans that the second book was on its way.

Some fans refused to wait. When *Harry Potter and the Chamber of Secrets* appeared in Britain in July 1998, thousands of young readers figured out how to order the Bloomsbury edition from Amazon.com's British site before it became available in the United States. Scholastic roared in protest, pointing out that only their company had the legal right to sell the book in the United States. Amazon countered that the Internet was revolutionizing the nature of business, including bookselling. Apparently unable to stem the tide of Potter-mania, Scholastic responded by moving

Rowling met with Queen Elizabeth at Bloomsbury's offices in London. One of the highest honors for a British citizen is to meet the queen.

up the publication date of Rowling's second novel from September to June 1999.

Young people were filled with anticipation: What would happen to Harry next? *Harry Potter and the Chamber of Secrets* opens as Harry finishes a particularly horrible summer at home with the Dursleys. He cannot wait to return to Hogwarts to begin his second year. Banished to his bedroom, he receives a visit from an elf named

Dobby who warns him not return to school after all, for great danger awaits him there. Nevertheless, Ron Weasley and his brothers free Harry from his prison bedroom with their flying car. Despite Dobby's warnings, Harry returns to Hogwarts and stumbles right into the mystery of the Chamber of Secrets.

On Halloween night, Harry, Ron, and Hermione find a message painted on a wall that reads, "The Chamber of Secrets has been opened. Enemies of the Heir, beware." The Chamber of Secrets, which had been sealed for 50 years, contains a deadly monster. The last time the chamber was opened, someone died. "The heir" in the message refers to a descendant of one of the school's four founders, Salazar Slytherin, who had an affinity for the dark side of magic. Apparently, only Slytherin's heir would be able to open the Chamber of Secrets and use the monster within to cleanse the school from all "muggle-borns" and "half-bloods" whom he believed were unworthy to study magic. Now that the Chamber is open again, fear reigns at Hogwarts as students who do not come from pureblood wizarding families are found petrified like stone statues. Harry and his friends must solve the mystery before the monster goes beyond merely petrifying its victims and kills again. Inevitably, Lord Voldemort takes a hand in trying to defeat Harry and his friends.

Readers were fascinated with the second book, and Harry Potter fever took hold. It seemed as though every child in the United States and England had a copy of Harry Potter in hand. By July 1999, just a month after the release of Rowling's second novel, there were 826,000 copies of *Harry Potter and the Sorcerer's Stone* and 915,000 copies of *Harry Potter and the Chamber of Secrets* in print.

Across the world, on beaches, at bedtime, in New York subways, and in their cars, kids read about Harry Potter. The magic of Harry Potter had become a phenomenon in publishing history.

In the third book, Harry Potter and the Prisoner of Azkaban, *Harry is 13 years old. Accordingly, he faces more mature problems, and gets into even scarier situations.*

6

A Phenomenon in Publishing

THE HARRY POTTER books are an unprecedented success and have topped bestseller lists. They have been translated into more than 60 languages and have sold more than 300 million copies worldwide.

There is a saying that "a rising tide floats all boats," which means that a positive force acts on all things that it can affect, big or small. By the time news of Rowling's third book, *Harry Potter and the Prisoner of Azkaban*, had reached youngsters, librarians, booksellers, and the media, the children's book publishing industry was beginning to feel the "rising tide" of Harry Potter and the enthusiasm it inspired.

By coincidence, another series aimed at young readers had just recently peaked in popularity. Earlier in the 1990s, Scholastic's paperback Goosebumps series attracted a huge following among readers age 8–12, especially boys. With titles like *Chicken, Chicken*; *Haunted Mask*; *Phantom of the Auditorium*; *Beware of the Purple Peanut Butter*; and *Please Don't Feed the Vampire,* author and former children's magazine editor R.L. Stine turned out short, easy-to-read, scary tales with a humorous twist. Stine could hardly write them fast enough, even at 20 pages a day. At one point, there were 57 books completed, another 42 planned, and 160 million copies in print. In 1997, about 6 million Goosebumps books sold each month in 15 different languages.

From a bookseller's point of view, however, R.L. Stine had a narrow impact on young people's reading interests. Kids who read Goosebumps did not necessarily want to read other books. Then, almost as quickly as Goosebumps had caught on, fans lost their taste for it. The ripple effect was that the children's paperback market dipped by almost 20 percent in the late 1990s. In 1999, the Association of American Publishers forecasted gloom for children's book sales. Actually, the association underestimated the percentage growth in children's hardcover sales by more than half. According to an association member who had helped develop the prediction, no one in bookselling had foreseen the arrival of Harry Potter. In 1999, Harry Potter accounted for much of the growth in children's literature: an increase in paperback sales of 24 percent to $660 million, and an increase in hardcover sales of 11 percent to $1.6 million.

The beauty of Harry Potter was that the quality of the writing and the story encouraged fans to find similar books. Booksellers were surprised: Never before had children come in, in such numbers, and requested comparable books. Major newspapers began to refer to the "halo effect" of Harry Potter. They suggested that young readers try books like the Redwall series by Brian Jacques, for example, as well as older titles in children's fantasy literature. Rowling mentioned that one of her favorite books as a child was Dodie Smith's 1948 book, *I Capture the Castle*, about 17-year-old Cassandra, who keeps a journal of life in a ramshackle English castle; the book's publisher, St. Martin's Press, immediately repackaged the book and included an endorsement from Rowling on the cover. The backlist title (meaning that it was an old book) steadily rose in sales from 11,000 to 54,000.

The boy with glasses and a broomstick had become a phenomenon in publishing. Confident that Rowling's appeal would stay strong, Scholastic debuted her third book, *Harry Potter and the Prisoner of Azkaban*, with a first-print run of 900,000 in the United States. Bloomsbury printed 275,000 for Britain and markets like Canada and Australia.

The third book is a little scarier than the first two. Harry is now 13 years old. The murderous and dreadful Sirius Black has escaped from Azkaban, the wizard prison, and Harry is believed to be his next victim. Soon, Black gains access into Hogwarts, even into Harry's own dormitory. Harry, Ron, and Hermione must figure out Sirius Black's original crime, whether he is connected to Harry's parents and their deaths, and whether Black is the traitor who betrayed Harry's parents to Voldemort. When he solves this puzzle, Harry finds both his father's best friends and his own godfather. Even though Harry, Ron, and Hermione do find the traitor, he escapes in the end, which leaves both Voldemort and one of his henchmen to torment Harry in the next volume.

Did you know...

American author Nancy K. Stouffer completed *The Legend of Rah and the Muggles* in 1984. In 2000, she sued Scholastic, claiming that Rowling's book infringed on her copyright. She cited, as one example, her use of the world *muggles*. The word, she said, came from her son's baby-talk word for cheeks. Rowling countered that her word *Muggles* came from a British word for fool. The word is in fact older than both writers. According to the *Chicago Sun-Times*, the Oxford English Dictionary traces the word back to the thirteenth century, when *muggles* meant "tails."* By the twentieth century, the word had become slang for marijuana, and in the 1920s, a marijuana user was called a mugglehead. In the 1930s, Louis Armstrong had a song called "Muggles," and in 1960, Carol Kendall's novel *The Gammage Cup*, a Newbery Award honor book, featured a character named Muggles. The U.S. District Court for southern New York ruled in favor of Rowling. They found not only that Rowling did not plagiarize the word *muggles*, but also that Stouffer had lied to the court and doctored evidence to support her claims. The court fined Stouffer $50,000 for this "pattern of intentional bad faith conduct."**

* Brenda Warner Rotzoll, "Disputed Harry Potter Word Boasts Long Literary Pedigree," *Chicago Sun-Times*, March 27, 2000.

** "Potter Author Zaps Court Rival," CNN.com World, September 19, 2002, http://archives.cnn.com/2002/WORLD/europe/UK/09/19/rowling.court/index.html.

When *Harry Potter and the Prisoner of Azkaban* was released in September 1999, all three titles in the Harry Potter series captured the first, second, and third slots on the *New York Times* bestseller list, and remained there for months afterward. By then, Rowling had also won the prestigious British Smarties Book Prize three years in a row, becoming the first author to do so. She requested that future Harry Potter titles not be considered for the award so that other authors could have a better chance to win. *Prisoner of Azkaban* also won the inaugural Whitbread Children's Book of the Year award. In 2000, the Queen honored Rowling by making her an Officer of the Order of the British Empire.

Rowling had never expected this kind of success or recognition. In an interview with Stephen Fry, she recalled her first book-signing in America. She had expected a few boys to come in, "with a scar penciled clumsily on their foreheads," but there were hundreds of people, young and old, and some of them dressed up in costumes. "I walked through this door, at the back of the store, and there were screams, literally screams, and flashbulbs going off." She admitted, "That was the closest I will ever get to being a pop star."[1]

Until her third book, Rowling had managed to avoid interviews. With media curiosity and even some controversy now swirling around the author and her books, she agreed to do interviews after the publication of *Harry Potter and the Prisoner of Azkaban*. The author turned out to be assertive, opinionated, and astute—not at all like the romantic image painted of her by the press. In fact, she resented being described again and again as a "penniless single mother," as she put it, who made good.

In a radio interview with the British Broadcasting System (BBC), Rowling addressed several issues about the Harry Potter books. First, there was a growing background rumble by some critics who argued that topics in her books such as evil, death, and murder were unsuitable for small children. She admitted that might be true, saying "I do think that, on occasion, the material is not suitable for six-year-olds. But you can't stop them reading it. . . . so I wouldn't say 'Don't read them [the books] to a six-year-old,' just be aware some of it does get uncomfortable." She added that the Harry Potter books deal with evil, and how evil it is to take a human life. "If you are going to write about those kinds of things," she said, "you have a moral obligation to show what that involves, not to prettify it or to minimize it."[2]

Rowling denied that she had hit on a formula for writing best-selling children's books, or that she knew what children wanted. "I sat down to write something I knew I would enjoy reading. I do not try to analyze it and I don't write to a formula. I always find it quite patronizing—'What do children want?'—as if they are a separate species. I do not write with an imaginary focus group of eight-year-olds in mind."[3]

Finally, Rowling voiced her unhappiness with newfound celebrity and the invasion of privacy that accompanies it. "When people start searching through your bins [garbage cans] it is horrible. It feels like such an invasion. I am not a politician, I am not an entertainer and I never expected this much interest in my life."[4]

With so much attention suddenly forced upon her, Rowling understandably felt considerable pressure as she worked on the fourth book in the series, *Harry Potter and the Goblet of Fire*. It would have to be the cornerstone book of the series, after all: the one that provided enough energy and new plot developments to propel the series forward for three more books. If the series flagged in the middle, disappointed readers might abandon Harry Potter by the millions.

Rowling worked 10-hour days to finish the manuscript as editors and sales people at Scholastic and Bloomsbury strategized about how to build excitement for the book. With the deadline approaching, Rowling saw that the story was much, much longer than she expected. Then, disaster struck as she discovered that something was wrong with the plot. Midway through the novel, Rowling realized that she had not set up events to reach the conclusion she wanted. It was as though she had built a house and then discovered that its size was bigger than the foundation. She had no choice but to start over.

Rowling finally submitted the finished manuscript to Bloomsbury. The Scholastic edition was 734 pages. Children's books usually are not more than 100 or 200 pages. Just how many kids were going to plow through something this long, with so many characters and strange names? Soon the world would find out. On July 8, 2000, *Harry Potter and the Goblet of Fire* arrived in bookstores amid an unprecedented amount of publicity for a children's book, or perhaps any book. In fact, British author Anthony Holden thought the attention was ridiculous and undeserved. In an opinion piece that appeared in *The Observer* in London, he complained, "Haven't Bloomsbury sold enough copies of J.K. Rowling's three volumes so far without resorting to advance hype worthy of a Wonderbra?" He called the books "Disney cartoons written in words, no more."[5] A week after his attack, the *Observer* published two pages of responses, mostly from young readers, that defended Rowling and accused Holden of jealousy.

An unsettling rumor began to circulate after nearly 3 million copies of the new book were in the hands of eager readers: There was a key mistake in the order in which Voldemort had killed people. During the battle between Voldemort and Harry in the climactic confrontation near the end of the fourth book, Harry forces the ghosts of all those whom Voldemort has killed with his wand to eject themselves momentarily into the living world. They emerge in the reverse order in which they were killed. First comes Cedric, the popular Hogwarts Quidditch player, whom Voldemort has most recently killed, then the groundskeeper of the Riddle Estate, then witch Bertha Jorkins, presumed to be missing, followed by Harry's parents.

Here is where there appears to be a mistake: Harry's father's ghost comes out first, followed by his mother's ghost. In the first book, Rowling makes clear that Harry's father died first, in an attempt to protect his wife and child. Harry's mother was then killed as she tried to protect Harry. If the ghosts of Voldemort's victims appear in reverse order, it seems that his mother's ghost should come out first and then his father's ghost. On her Web site, Rowling later confirmed that Lily should have emerged first, then James. She blamed the error on the last-minute editing required by the book's tight deadline.

In *Harry Potter and the Goblet of Fire*, the first 75 pages mainly review important events in the first three books. Nearly 1,000 printed pages of story have preceded this volume, so it is as though Rowling wants to make certain her readers are prepared for her longest title yet. The new information readers discover is that Voldemort is on the move again. Meanwhile, Harry escapes his summer imprisonment at the Dursleys' to attend the Quidditch World

Executives of the People's Literature Publishing House in Beijing show the new Harry Potter book translated into Chinese, further proof of Harry Potter's universal appeal.

Cup with the Weasley family and Hermione. Thousands of international witches and wizards have gathered at the Cup. Chaos erupts when the "Dark Mark," Voldemort's sign, appears in the sky.

As he returns to Hogwarts for his fourth year, Harry finds that only a few of his classmates are concerned about the Dark Mark. Everyone is more interested in news of the Triwizard Tournament, a contest between the wizard champions of Hogwarts, Durmstrang, and Beauxbatons, the three largest schools of magic. Harry is still too young to be chosen as Hogwarts' official school champion, but someone finds a way to enter him in the contest anyway. Perhaps this is a compliment, or maybe it is a trick. Once chosen, Harry *must* participate. It soon became clear that the person who entered his name intended to harm him.

During the year-long competition, champions complete three magical tasks with the hope that they will win honor for their school and a monetary prize for themselves. There is a connection between the Dark Mark seen in the sky and the Triwizard Tournament, and something is suspicious about the new professor for Defense Against the Dark Arts. Hermione finds her own cause in the form of liberating the house elves from what she considers to be slavery. Everyone close to Harry gets annoyed with muckraking journalist Rita Skeeter, who seems determined to ruin his life.

Once the Triwizard Tournament ends with a twist, and the victory celebration is underway, Harry is drawn into another battle with Voldemort. Rowling delivers on her promise that a well-liked character will die. Harry escapes with his life, but the end of this story spells more-than-usual concern for the future, because Voldemort has regained his body, which he had lost when he tried to kill infant Harry. As the book ends, Professor Dumbledore implores the international wizarding community to stand united against the dark side.

Said film and book critic Janet Maslin of the *New York Times*, "As the midpoint in a projected seven-book series, *Goblet of Fire* is exactly the big, clever, vibrant, tremendously assured installment that gives shape and direction to the whole undertaking and still somehow preserves the material's enchanting innocence."[6]

Death figures prominently in the fourth book. It was somewhat more difficult and stressful for Rowling to write *Goblet of Fire* because she had never "killed" a character before. Since the series began with the deaths of Harry's parents, however, death has always been an issue. Another troublesome point when she wrote this book, Rowling explained, was her development of Rita Skeeter, the nosy journalist with little respect for the truth or people's privacy. Rowling had planned the character of Rita Skeeter long before she started on the fourth book. Rowling did not know that "by the time I wrote book four I would have met quite a lot of Ritas and people would assume that I was writing Rita in response to what had happened to me," she said, referring to how a few journalists had hounded her or distorted the facts of her life. She decided to go ahead with the character and risk a possible backlash from the media. Once she made this decision, Rowling admitted "that writing Rita was a lot more fun having met a few people I had met."[7]

By August 2000, *Harry Potter and the Goblet of Fire* joined Rowling's three other titles on the *New York Times* bestseller list. Rowling's books dominated the 68-year-old list, so editors at the *New York Times* decided it was time for a change and created a bestseller list specifically for children's books. On the new list, Harry Potter took the top 4 spots, followed by 11 other children's and young adult titles. Publishers were divided on whether or not a children's book list was a good idea.

"It's been a long time coming," remarked Joanna Cotler, publisher of Joanna Cotler Books at HarperCollins Children's, "and I'm thrilled that Harry Potter is what finally pushed them into it. I've always looked at the *New York Times'* best-seller list as wonderful free advertising. Now children's books get it, too."[8] Barbara Marcus, president of the Scholastic Children's Book Group, J.K. Rowling's American publisher, disagreed. To her, the success of Harry Potter annoyed other publishers, so the *New York Times* banished children's books to their own list. "The *Times* became a spoiler of it all. I always believed that bestseller lists are just that, and they should be recording and *reporting* the bestselling books in the country," Marcus told Salon.com.[9]

Rowling tries to stay away from the controversy and fame created by Harry Potter as much as possible. To this day, she treasures being able to walk down a winding medieval street in Edinburgh unnoticed. As a private person, Rowling is also very ordered, reserved, and in control. She claims that her personal life is not very interesting. Although Rowling is now a famous writer, she does not feel like a celebrity. Despite the interviews and photographs and millions of fans, Rowling spends much of her day alone at her desk, writing. Most of her free time goes into caring for her family. In 2001, Rowling married Neil Murray, an anesthetist (a doctor who administers anesthetics). They have a son, David Gordon, who was born on March 3, 2003, and a daughter, Mackenzie, who was born in January 2005, plus Rowling's daughter from her first marriage.

Rowling's life is very busy, and she has little time for hobbies. As she told audiences, "I have no spare time at all. When I'm not writing or looking after the children, I read and sleep."[10] Even with her busy schedule, Rowling continues to be a big reader. She reads mostly novels and biographies. Her favorite writer of all time is Jane Austen, one of the most influential novelists of the early nineteenth century.

In addition to the loss of her privacy, Rowling's fame has created other challenges. When her daughter Jessica was still only five or six, for instance, classmates quizzed her relentlessly about Harry Potter and refused to believe that her mother had not read her the books (which she really had not done). Rowling told school authorities that Jessica needed to be left alone. When she discovered that Jessica had asked other children about Harry Potter, however, she decided that it was time to read the books to her. Fortunately, Jessica, like millions of other children, loved her mother's books.

In 2004, the University of Edinburgh conferred an honorary doctorate on J.K. Rowling. The university's vice chancellor, Professor Timothy O'Shea, is shown here applauding Rowling.

7

Breaking Records

WHEN ROWLING TURNED in the manuscript for *Harry Potter and the Sorcerer's Stone*, she never dreamed that she would one day achieve this kind of success, popularity, or wealth.

One unanticipated dilemma of being the most popular children's author in the world involves money. Rowling is one of the richest women in Britain. Actually, she is one of the richest women in the world. Her first 5 books have sold an estimated 270 million copies worldwide in 62 languages. In 2004, she landed on *Forbes'* list of the world's richest people. According to *Forbes*, she is one of only five self-made female billionaires, and the first billion-dollar author. Rowling says the extent of her sudden wealth makes her somewhat uncomfortable. She has gone from struggling writer to billionaire in a relatively short period of time.

"Yes, I'm riddled with guilt," Rowling admits about her wealth. "It's a very weird situation. Then again, there is a solution. You can give it away. You can't sit there and say, 'Ah, it's tragic, I've got a lot of money,' because nobody's stopping you spreading it about a bit."[1] So she contributes to the work of the Multiple Sclerosis Society of Scotland in memory of her mother. In addition, the formerly jobless parent of an infant daughter is also the ambassador for the National Council for One Parent Families in Britain.

In 2001, Rowling contributed more money to charities directly through two booklets: *Fantastic Beasts and Where to Find Them* and *Quidditch Through the Ages*. Rowling wrote these booklets, which appear as the titles of Harry's school books within the novels, for the U.K. fundraiser Comic Relief, which also asked best-selling British authors Delia Smith and Helen Fielding to contribute booklets. For each book sold, approximately 80 percent of the cover price would go toward combating poverty and social inequality around the globe. The books have raised about $30 million for the fund.

In January 2006, Rowling went to Bucharest, Romania, to raise funds for the Children's High Level Group, an organization that helps to enforce the human rights of children, especially in eastern Europe. She also read at an event with authors Stephen King and John Irving at Radio City Music Hall in New York City. The profits were donated to the Haven Foundation, a charity that helps artists whose accidents or illnesses have left them uninsured and unable to work. The reading also benefited *Médecins Sans Frontières*/Doctors Without Borders, an international independent organization that delivers emergency aid to people affected by armed conflict, epidemics, natural or manmade disasters, or exclusion from health care in more than 70 countries. Rowling received an honorary Doctor of Laws (LL.D.) degree from the University of Aberdeen for her significant contribution to many charitable causes and to society.

Her new wealth, of course, also carries benefits. The best thing about it, Rowling has said, is that she no longer has to worry about bills. She lives quite comfortably and owns three properties. In 2001, she purchased a luxurious nineteenth-century estate on the banks of the River Tay, near Aberfeldy, in Perth and Kinross, Scotland, which she describes as a peaceful place where she can be with her family. She also owns a home in Morningside, Edinburgh, as well as a Georgian house in London. Still, she hopes that her family can live a "normal" life. Rowling explains that, despite her wealth,

> There are no plans on either of our parts [her and Neil's] to stop working, put our feet up and go yachting around the world or anything, pleasant though that would be and does seem sometimes. We keep working and I think that's a pretty good example to set for your children; that whatever money you might make, self-worth really lies in finding out what you do best. It's doing your proper job, isn't it?[2]

In addition to the Harry Potter books, the films have also been extremely successful. Warner Bros. purchased the film rights to the first two novels for a seven-figure sum in

October 1998. The films, released in 2001 and 2002, were both directed by Chris Columbus (*Home Alone*, 1990 and *Mrs. Doubtfire*, 1993). The 2004 film of *Harry Potter and the Prisoner of Azkaban* was directed by Alfonso Cuarón, whose films include *A Little Princess* (1995) and *Children of Men* (2006). Director Mike Newell (*Donnie Brasco*, 1997 and *Mona Lisa Smile*, 2003) directed *Harry Potter and the Goblet of Fire*, the fourth film. In the summer of 2007, *Harry Potter and the Order of the Phoenix*, the movie version of the fifth book, was released; it was directed by David Yates, a British television director.

Warner Bros. has allowed Rowling to have much input in the direction of the films, which is unusual in Hollywood. She has helped Steve Kloves write the scripts, and has made certain stipulations about the production of the movies. One of her principal stipulations was that the films must be shot in Britain with an all-British cast. The famous director Steven Spielberg decided not to direct the first film, possibly because of Rowling's demands, as the press claimed. Rowling denies this on her Web site. For the first film, Rowling required that Coca-Cola, who won the right to tie their products to the film series, donate $18 million to the American charity Reading Is Fundamental—an unprecedented move.

Rowling is happy with all of the films and admires the actors very much. Once in an online interview with Scholastic, someone asked if she would ever have a cameo in a Harry Potter movie. "No, definitely not. I hate watching myself on-screen!" Rowling responded.[3]

The first four Harry Potter books were tremendous successes. What kind of response would the final three receive? Fans were eager to find out. The Harry Potter books always end with some kind of cliffhanger, which leaves readers hungry for the next one. Fans had been waiting for the continuation of Harry's story since 2000; three years had gone by, and their appetites were whetted.

The fifth book, *Harry Potter and the Order of the Phoenix,* was released in 2003. Longer than any of Rowling's previous books, the book runs 870 pages. A few critics complained that the pacing of the novel is too slow at first, but most critics gave the book supportive reviews. "As Harry gets older, Rowling gets better," wrote John Leonard in the *New York Times*.[4] In this book, Harry is growing up and begins to lose his innocent and boyish illusions. He is a realistic teenager, and has become more moody and sullen. At 15 years old, Harry has fits of rage, a major crush, and a desire to rebel. The fifth book is much darker, and it is also more of a coming-of-age novel than the previous four.

Harry faces an overwhelming course load as the fifth year students prepare for their Ordinary Wizarding Levels examinations, suffer disappointing changes in the Gryffindor Quidditch team lineup, and have a dreadful new Defense Against the Dark Arts teacher. Harry also has vivid dreams about long hallways and closed doors, which increase pain in his lightning-shaped scar. Harry confronts death again, and also learns of a startling prophecy. As Rowling promised, in this book, a character close to Harry dies.

Rowling became pregnant with her third child as she was writing the sixth book, *Harry Potter and the Half-Blood Prince*, and she often joked about them racing each other into the world. She assured her fans the book would still be written. The sixth book is dedicated to Mackenzie: "My beautiful daughter, I dedicate / Her ink-and-paper twin."

The sixth novel was published in 2005. This novel explores Lord Voldemort's past, as Harry prepares for the final battle amidst emerging romantic relationships. Would this book live up to its predecessors' popularity?

Did you know...

Rowling made a special guest appearance as herself on the hit cartoon show *The Simpsons* in the fourth episode of the fifteenth season. Other guests on this episode include Prime Minister Tony Blair and Sir Ian McKellen. On the episode, the Simpson family is visiting England. Lisa sees Rowling outside of a bookstore.

LISA: Look! It's J.K. Rowling, author of the Harry Potter books! You've turned a generation of kids on to reading.

J.K. ROWLING: Thank you, young Muggle.

LISA: Can you tell me what happens at the end of the series?

J.K. ROWLING: (sigh) He grows up and marries you. Is that what you want to hear?

LISA: (dreamily) Yes.

Rowling made a special guest appearance as herself on the animated show The Simpsons. *Above, the animation of Rowling is shown second from left; the character on the far left is Queen Elizabeth II.*

In 24 hours, the book sold 6.9 million copies in the United States alone. It generated over $100 million in sales on its opening weekend, outpacing even the combined take of the top movies at the box office that same weekend. Like the other books, with the sixth one, *Harry Potter and the Half-Blood Prince*, there were midnight bookstore openings, special events, and wild publicity. The hype was endless, including a glittering ceremony at midnight in Edinburgh, the city in which Rowling wrote the first book.

More so than any of the previous books, fans of the sixth book were divided. The sixth book is much darker, and Rowling has said that it should be regarded as the first half of a two-volume work. Some fans were disappointed that Harry and Hermione did not develop a romance, although other fans argued that this had been clear from the beginning. Romance is a major part of the book, however, as several other relationships unfold.

Rowling said, "I'm aware that *Half-Blood Prince* will not delight everyone, because it does shoot down some theories. A few people won't particularly like it, and a lot of people aren't going to like the death very much, but that was always what was planned to come."[5]

For the most part, critics were impressed, and gave the book strong reviews. In the *New York Times*, Liesl Schillinger wrote, "Rowling has succeeded in delivering another spellbinding fantasy set in her consummately well-imagined alternate reality."[6] A movie based on the sixth book is scheduled to be released in November 2008.

To date, all seven of the Harry Potter books have broken sales records. More than 250 million books in the Harry Potter series have been sold in some 61 translations (including Latin, Welsh, Ancient Greek, and Irish) in more than 200 countries. The sixth book even made it into *Guinness World Records* for being the fastest-selling book ever. The seventh book, *Harry Potter and the Deathly Hallows*, broke even *Goblet of Fire*'s records: On the first day of sales, *Deathly Hallows* sold 11 million copies in the United States and the United Kingdom, compared to 9 million for *Goblet of Fire*. Barnes and Noble, the largest U.S. book chain, reported all-time record sales of 560,000 copies sold in the first hour—more than 150 copies per second.

Harry (Daniel Radcliffe), Ron (Rupert Grint), and Hermione (Emma Watson) walk beside the Hogwarts Express in the 2007 movie version of Harry Potter and the Order of the Phoenix.

8

Creating
Harry's World

J.K. ROWLING HAS PUBLISHED seven Harry Potter books within a decade, which is more than 4,000 pages combined. The intricate plot lines and many characters could be confusing, but Rowling was very careful with her plotting and outlining. She tended to work on one book at a time. "During the first five years that I was writing the series, I made plans and wrote small pieces of all the books," she explained. But later she said, "I concentrate on one book at a time, though occasionally I will get an idea for a future book and scribble it down for future reference."[1] Her original plan for the seven books changed some in details, but for the most part, the basic plan stayed the same. When Rowling worked on a book, she discussed it with no one. She claimed this was not to protect the property, but "because I think if you discuss the work while you're doing it you tend to dissipate the energy you need to do it."[2]

Although it was hard work to write the Harry Potter books, it was a lot of fun. Rowling created fantastical places, magic, and potions, along with a multitude of characters and a mythical population. Critic John Leonard of the *New York Times* lists the many fantastic inhabitants in the world of Potter:

> Thus a multiethnic multiculture of warlocks, mermaids, mugwumps, trolls, vampires, fairies, dwarfs, ghouls, mummies, pixies, gnomes, banshees, wood nymphs, dementors, boggarts, veelas, animagi and parselmouths. And a colorful bestiary of gargoyles, gorgons, ravens, mandrakes, manticores, stags, porlocks, kneazles, crups, knarls, griffins, bubotubers, flobberworms, grindylows (water demons), hunkypunks (bog sirens), three-headed dogs, bat-winged horses, map-reading cats, ferret-eating hippogriffs and blast-ended skrewts. And a rich diet of eels' eyes, bat spleens, ice mice, butterbeer, armadillo bile, nosebleed nougat, pickled slug, fizzing whizbees, powdered root of asphodel, powdered spine of lionfish, powdered horn of unicorn and shredded skin of boomslang.[3]

At the same time, what makes this world so approachable to readers is that much of it also takes place in a domestic, everyday setting, infused with the magical. As Liesl Schillinger writes, "Her [Rowling's] fantasy world looks so much like home."[4] For example, the Hogwarts School for Witchcraft and Wizardry is a haunted castle, with secret passageways, ghosts, monsters, and moving portraits, and yet it also a place where students face boring teachers and difficult exams.

How did Rowling come up with all of this: the potions, the magic, the plot, and the characters? She obviously has a creative, rich, and active imagination. She does not live in a bubble, however, and like most writers, she has been influenced by others. Although Rowling herself is not a big fan of fantasy books in general, she acknowledges that fairy tales and myths have influenced her. For the Harry Potter books, Rowling sometimes took variations of stories and words from folklore and mythology. From time to time, she might look through books, such as *The Dictionary of Phrase and Fable*, but often what inspired her, including when she was creating names, was something by chance, something she stumbled across in general reading. Humor is also a major element of Harry Potter. Rowling loves comedy, and her work has probably been influenced by Monty Python, one of her favorite British comedies.

Rowling finds that it is both fun and difficult to name characters, spells, and potions. For example, when she was writing the *Half-Blood Prince,* she needed a name for another potion. "I sat for ten minutes at the keyboard then I just typed 'X.' I thought, 'I'll go back and fill that in later.' Sometimes you really want to get on with the story. Sometimes names just come to you, which is great feeling, but sometimes it is difficult and you have to batter your brain for a while."[5] Most of the magic is made up. She also uses an abundance of Latin in the books; most of her knowledge of the ancient language is self-taught.

When Rowling writes, she sees the images in her head first, very clearly, and then she attempts to describe what she sees. Sometimes, she draws the images of the characters or places for her own amusement. Rowling loves to write, and when she has the time, she tries to do it all day, or sometimes all evening. It is fairly uncommon, however, to have that stretch of time with three children. In an interview in 2000, Rowling said that she had the most fun writing *The Prisoner of Azkaban.* Then, in 2004, Rowling said the sixth book, which she was working on at the time, was the most fun. Maybe now it is the seventh book.

Rowling has many favorite characters, including Harry, Hermione, Ron, Hagrid, and Dumbledore. She explained that she loves to write about Snape, "even though he is not always the nicest person."[6] She also likes Lupin, and one of her newest favorites is Luna. Although Rowling does not know exactly how many characters she has created, she thinks that she is close to 200. It is interesting to note that, when Rowling writes, she continues to see the characters as she first imagined them, rather than as the actors in the movies. "I was writing them far too long before the films came out for the film images to dispel what's in my head. I was lucky in that sense. I'd lived with these characters so long, it just couldn't have any effect."[7]

Rowling also likes to write dialogue, and her books have translated very well to audiobooks. British-born actor Jim Dale has been the voice of the Rowling audiobooks in the United States. He has devoted more than 100 hours of time to the recordings, with different voices for the many characters. Listening Library publisher Tim Ditlow selected Dale in part because his English accent has been tempered by living in the United States since 1980. American children sometimes find very strong English accents difficult to understand, Ditlow says.[8]

Rowling feels proud of the Harry Potter books, but she admits that it is difficult for her to read them after they have

Rowling talks with one of the winners of the essay contest "How the Harry Potter Books Have Changed My Life." Many credit Rowling with making reading fun for young children as well as rejuvenating sales of other children's books.

been published. This is often typical of published authors. "When I re-read the books, I often catch myself re-editing them. It's an uncomfortable experience," she says. "However, the more time elapses, the less I find myself doing that—I can now read *Sorcerer's Stone* fairly comfortably."[9] For the most part, she does not read the books once they have been published, except to check a fact. Rowling admits, "Therefore there are thousands of fans who know the books much better than I do. My one advantage is I know what's going to happen, and I've got a lot of back-story."[10] The backstory explains much about the characters and their histories, and it does not necessarily show up in the books. Rowling has boxes filled with the many note-books of backstory that she has written.

Rowling's typical fans are extremely dedicated. Many have even read the lengthy books more than once, examin-ing plot lines, clues, and hints. At readings and talks that

Did you know...

In early July 2005, Real Canadian Super-store, a chain of markets in British Columbia, Canada, accidentally sold several copies of *The Half-Blood Prince* before the authorized release date. The Canadian publisher, Raincoast Books, obtained an injunction from the Supreme Court of British Columbia that forbade the purchasers from reading the books or from discussing the contents before the official release date. The publisher offered buy-ers a Harry Potter t-shirt and a bookplate signed by J.K. Rowling if they returned their copies before July 16, the release date. The *Globe and Mail* news-paper then stated that they planned to post a review of the book at 12:01 A.M. local time. Raincoast responded by saying that they would view such an act as a violation of the trade secret injunction. The injunction sparked a number of news articles alleg-ing that the injunction had restricted fundamental rights. Several people called for a boycott, request-ing that Raincoast Books issue an apology. Instead, the publisher reached a compromise with the paper so that a review could appear the next morning.

Rowling has given, the children in the audience often ask detailed questions about characters, plots, or even particular lines. Some of these kids have practically memorized the books. Rowling fans are loyal and curious. There are many Web sites and chat rooms devoted to Rowling and the Harry Potter books. Two particularly well-known Web sites are MuggleNet (www.mugglenet.com), and the Leaky Cauldron (www.the-leaky-cauldron.org). The fans who run these sites—Emerson Spartz and Melissa Anelli, respectively—have had the chance to meet and talk with Rowling. Rowling also has an official Web site, where she publishes diary entries and answers to frequently asked questions.

In many available Harry Potter chat rooms on the Internet, Potter fans discuss theories and rumors about Rowling and her books. At this point, Rowling has stopped reading most of the online chatter and theory about the books. "Some of it is funny, some of it is weird, and some is just downright crazy."[11] Rowling also receives many fan letters, from both girls and boys. She receives between 800 and 1,000 letters every week. The fans who have had the opportunity to meet Rowling or hear her read know that she is down-to-earth, friendly, and engaging. Rowling does not view herself as a celebrity. She is modest, and although she sometimes bristles when confronted by Rita Skeeter–like journalists, with her young fans she is tender and funny. She encourages children to read as much as possible, and not to limit themselves to reading only Harry Potter books. Rowling is a hopeful person who has strong personal values. She has said that, if there were one thing she could change about the world, "I would make each and every one of us much more tolerant."[12]

Meanwhile, Pottermania continued. After the sixth book, fans asked and made bets about what would happen in the seventh book. Before the book was released, Rowling had revealed that at least two characters would die in the final book, one of whom might be Harry himself. She also divulged that the book would feature the long-awaited final confrontation between Harry and Lord Voldemort. Authors Stephen King and John Irving asked Rowling not to kill off Harry in Book 7 during a press conference, but Rowling remained silent on the issue.

Rowling admits that it was an intense feeling to write the last book. "It feels scary, actually. It's been 15 years. Can you imagine? One of the longest adult relationships of my life."[13] On December 19, 2006, she updated her fans on the progress of the seventh book on her Web site:

> The long lack of updates has been due to some very hard work. I'm now writing scenes that have been planned, in some cases, for a dozen years or even more. I don't think anyone who has not been in a similar situation can possibly know how this feels: I am alternately elated and overwrought. I both want, and don't want, to finish this book (don't worry, I will.) [14]

In the months before the seventh book was released, speculation about its contents ran wild on the Internet. Fans debated details about the plot and characters, and made guesses about how things would be tied up.

Scholastic, the publisher, contributed to the giddy anticipation by launching a multi-million dollar marketing campaign called "There Will Soon Be 7." This included a "Knight Bus," which traveled to 40 libraries in the United States; online fan discussions and competitions; and collectible bookmarks and tattoos. At the Scholastic headquarters in New York City, a "Harry Potter Place" was created, with festivities including a 20-foot-high Whomping Willow, face painting, fire-eaters, magicians, and more.

Three days before the release, Rowling made a plea on her Web site for fans to ignore all of the misinformation that was popping up on the Web, and asking everyone to preserve the secrecy of the plot. Publisher Bloomsbury invested a substantial amount of money to attempt to keep the book's contents secure until the release date. Despite this, 759 pages were leaked to the Internet prior to the official release—the most serious security breach in the Harry Potter series' history.

Finally, on July 21, 2007, *Harry Potter and the Deathly Hallows* was released in the United States and the United Kingdom. *Deathly Hallows* broke records as the fastest selling book ever, selling more than 11 million copies in its first 24 hours in the stores. It was released globally in 93 countries. After the release, Rowling went on a U.S. book tour, her first since 2000. The seventh book received generally positive reviews, and most critics were careful not to spoil the ending.

Rowling had completed the manuscript while staying at the Balmoral Hotel in Edinburgh in January 2007. She left a signed statement on a marble bust of Hermes in her hotel room that read, "J.K. Rowling finished writing *Harry Potter and the Deathly Hallows* in this room (652) on 11 January 2007." She has said that the last chapter of the book, however, was written very early in the creation of the series, probably around 1990. Rowling reported that she felt happy with the last book and has claimed it as her favorite. Rowling's fans were happy with the book, too, though it was bittersweet: after reading the *Deathly Hallows*, they would have to say good-bye to Harry Potter.

The last book in the series, Harry Potter and the Deathly Hallows, *made quite a sensation when it was released in July 2007. In addition to finishing up the main story, the book contains an epilogue describing what happens to Harry, Ron, and Hermione as adults.*

9

Harry's Place in Children's Literature

WHEN ANYTHING ARTISTIC—a television program, a movie, a CD of songs, a fashion craze, or a book—becomes popular, it invites analysis. People naturally want to identify why something is popular because it might shed light on what matters to us as human beings. Classic love songs are said to capture certain universal feelings of love, for example. Great movies with serious themes are often praised for dramatizing emotional conflicts in people's lives.

Likewise, the Harry Potter books have not escaped analysis. How could they when millions of children on several continents have read them, and will continue to read them? Books that have so directly influenced the reading tastes of young people and appeal to them so strongly are certain to be analyzed on many different levels.

The Harry Potter books are first judged on a literary level, because they are stories, after all. As a storyteller, Rowling has been called a fine stylist and a clever fantasist. An editor of the *Times Literary Supplement* in London expressed the opinion of many critics that, as engaging stories with positive themes, Rowling's books deserved to be liked. "It takes an extremely curmudgeonly attitude to despise these books," he wrote.[1]

On the other hand, other critics who apply stricter standards for judging literature have not been as complimentary. In a *Wall Street Journal* article, Harold Bloom, Sterling Professor of Humanities at Yale University, said of Rowling's writing, "Her prose style, heavy on clichés, makes no demands upon her readers."[2] Robert McCrum, the literary editor of *The Observer*, wrote a review that otherwise praised Rowling as a storyteller, but he added, "Her work . . . has the reader by the throat from page to page, but her prose is as flat (and as English) as old beer."[3]

In Rowling's defense, other reviewers have argued that the fact that adults enjoy her books does not mean that her books should be measured against adult literature. After all, the Harry Potter books are written for children. Nationally syndicated columnist William Safire went further and scolded adults for "buying these books ostensibly to read to kids, but actually to read for themselves. . . . [T]his is not just dumbing down; it is growing down. The purpose of reading, once you get the hang of it, is not merely to follow the action of a plot, but to learn about characters, explore different ideas and enter other minds."[4]

Even when compared with other books for children, Harry Potter sometimes comes in second. After the ballots were counted to award Britain's Carnegie Medal, Britain's most prestigious award for children's books, Annie Everall, the head of the 12-member judging panel, announced the panels' conclusions just before *Goblet of Fire* was published. She said that the opinion of the panel was that the characters in Harry Potter were "more one-dimensional" than those in the rival books for the prize.

Debates like these over the literary merits of Harry Potter have not kept the books out of any child's hands, of course. Many critics praise the books, with reviewers pointing out that the characters become more developed and complex with each book in the series, particularly the fifth and sixth books. Whether or not critics agree on Rowling's abilities as a stellar novelist, her millions of young readers serve

Did you know...

In the wake of recent airline restrictions, Rowling was almost prevented from boarding a flight home from New York when she refused to let the manuscript for the final book of the series out of her sight. She would not place the manuscript in her check-in baggage, for fear that the work would be lost or secrets would be leaked. Officials at the airport, however, thought it should not be allowed as part of her carry-on luggage. Rowling claimed that if she had not been allowed to take her notes onboard her flight, she would have sailed back to the United Kingdom. The security guards finally relented.

as proof that she succeeds the world over as a much-loved storyteller. A far more serious challenge to the Harry Potter books has come from another set of critics who object to what the books rely on: the concept of magic.

No well-known group or organization has stepped forward and mounted a campaign against the Harry Potter books, but objections tend to follow a pattern. Although it seemed as if most adults were happy that kids were reading, there have been parents and groups in the United States who see the books as "dangerous" for promoting witches and the occult. Focus on the Family, a fundamentalist conservative Christian group, is specific: "The danger of Rowling's books is the fact that, though witches and wizards aren't portrayed *realistically,* they (at least the 'good' ones) are portrayed *positively.*"[5] The group fears "desensitization to witchcraft," meaning that young people may be encouraged to accept it as normal.

It is worth noting that self-proclaimed witches have not rushed to embrace the Harry Potter books, either. "It really doesn't have anything to do with us," said a Wiccan priest who lives in Plymouth, England. "I've read these books, since I wanted to see what was in them before I gave them to my kids, and I must say that these books no more promote witchcraft than *Anne of Green Gables* promotes moving to Nova Scotia."[6]

Asked whether an author should have a moral sense of responsibility when it comes to children, Rowling has said that when she writes, she does not think specifically about a moral lesson she wants to teach. She has also said the objections to magic and wizardry in her work miss the point anyway. The books are not so much about magic as they are about the freedom of imagination and about developing one's full potential. The beauty of reading is, as with

C.S. Lewis, "to jump into these different pools to enter different worlds," points out Rowling.[7]

Rowling believes it is dangerous that so many adults object to what children read. She comments, "I feel very strongly that there is a move to sanitize literature. Because we're trying to protect children, not from . . . the grisly facts of life, but from their own imaginations."[8]

Young adult novelist Judy Blume, author of *Are You There God? It's Me, Margaret*; *Tales of Fourth Grade Nothing*; and many other books, wrote an editorial in the *New York Times,* defending the Harry Potter books. Her basic message is that reading is good for children, and that parents should encourage their kids to read, not take the books out of their hands. No stranger to the world of book banning, as many of her own titles have been challenged, Blume wrote, "The real danger is not in the books, but in laughing off those who would ban them. The protests against Harry Potter follow a tradition that has been growing since the early 1980s and often leaves school principals trembling with fear that is then passed down to teachers and librarians."[9]

The American Library Association (ALA) reported in 2006 that books in the Harry Potter series were the most frequently challenged of the twenty-first century. There were more than 3,000 attempts to remove books from schools and public libraries between 2000 and 2005. Challenges are defined as formal, written complaints filed with a library or school requesting that materials be removed because of content or appropriateness. Most likely, there have been many more challenges that go unreported. Judith F. Krug, director of the ALA office for intellectual freedom, responds to these parents: "What book did you read? Or did you read it at all?"[10]

On her Web site, under "News," Rowling responded:

Once again, the Harry Potter books feature on this year's list of most-banned books. As this puts me in the company of Harper Lee, Mark Twain, J. D. Salinger, William Golding, John Steinbeck and other writers I revere, I have always taken my annual inclusion on the list as a great honour. "Every burned book enlightens the world."—Ralph Waldo Emerson.[11]

The *New York Times* critic John Leonard also weighs in on the issue, stating that "any series that celebrates courage, friendship, owls and brooms does more good than harm."[12]

For the most part, parents, teachers, librarians, and publishers around the world seem thrilled that children are reading so much. One important reason the Potter books are so popular may be because they reassure and encourage children to use their imaginations, as well as to develop their full potential. All young people wonder at some time or another whether they are special in some way. At the very beginning of *Harry Potter and the Sorcerer's Stone*, Harry, too, has a moment of doubt about whether he has what it takes to become a wizard.

Scholastic vice president Arthur A. Levine, who purchased the rights to publish Harry Potter in the United States for the highest amount ever bid for a foreign children's book, knew why the story appealed to him. "The thing I loved the most about reading Harry Potter," said Levine, "is the idea of growing up unappreciated, feeling outcast and then this great satisfaction of being discovered. That is the fantasy of every person who grows up feeling marginalized in any way."[13]

Film critic A.O. Scott offered similar personal reasons. "You feel, somehow, that they [the books] have always been there, waiting for you to discover. You also feel, in spite of being one of several million crazed fans, that they were written for you alone, a wizard stranded in an uncomprehending Muggle world, waiting for someone to recognize that what everyone else calls your abnormalities are really powers."[14]

The books have certainly worked to get kids to read. "Harry Potter really got my daughter reading—she didn't read books before and now she loves it,'' said Lorraine Stern, waiting in line with her daughter to buy *Harry Potter and the Goblet of Fire*. Her daughter, Hannah, 11, said: "At school, everybody comes up to each other asking, 'Did you read the new Harry Potter?' If I didn't get it this weekend, I'd be really mad."[15]

"There has never been anything like this is the history of book selling," said Steve Riggio, vice chairman of Barnes & Noble. "I think this could be the most profitable book we ever sold; if we can get kids hooked on a seven-book series, hopefully we could get them hooked on reading for life."[16]

Where do the Harry Potter books stand in the world of children's literature? Will they become classics?

In C.S. Lewis's *The Chronicles of Narnia* (1956), children move back and forth between reality and fantasy worlds using magic. They are able to fight evil wherever they find it, in this world or another one. A few adults or authority figures can be trusted around magic, but most are too unimaginative, mean, or incompetent to be dependable, which is a repeated theme in young people's fantasy literature. Other well-known books in this vein include Lewis Carroll's *Alice's Adventures in Wonderland* (1865), L. Frank Baum's *The Wizard of Oz*, and Ursula K. Le Guin's *The Wizard of Earthsea* (1968).

Then there is Harry Potter. Where do Rowling's books fit in the long line of fantasy books written for young people?

Rowling poses with her husband, Neil Murray, before the premiere of the movie Harry Potter and the Order of the Phoenix. *The two married in a private ceremony in December 2001, after an attempt to marry in July was thwarted when the press learned of it.*

Are they something new, or do they draw on themes, conflicts, and settings that have fascinated young readers for a long time?

To begin with, Rowling's use of magic continues a tradition that is as old as beanstalks, witches, enchanted forests, and potions. From the very beginning of *Harry Potter and the Sorcerer's Stone*, readers plunge into a reality outside the normal one. In the first chapter, sorcerers Dumbledore and Professor McGonagall meet on a suburban street and discuss amazing events. A deadly battle has taken place between wizards, and an exceptional child named Harry has somehow survived! Not many pages later, Harry and Rowling's readers joyously leave the humdrum world of Privet Drive behind as they depart for the world of magic from platform nine and three-quarters at King's Cross station.

Rowling also develops her books using another long-standing tradition in young people's literature: settings in which young characters live among their peers. In Harry's case, it is Hogwarts School of Witchcraft and Wizardry. More than a century ago, Rudyard Kipling made popular a school setting for the adventures of boys who outwitted their teachers in *Stalky & Co.*, which became a model for countless other authors. Schools make excellent stages for drama. In Robert Cormier's *The Chocolate War* (1974), the boring adult world barely exists beyond the walls of Trinity High School. Inside the school, right clashes with wrong practically every day.

Rowling is writing for young readers, so the challenges of relying on oneself and growing up are central to her books, which is at the heart of all first-rate literature for young people. It would be hard to find a book that won the Newbery award for children's literature, for instance, such as Richard Peck's *A Year Down Yonder* (2001) or Christopher Paul Curtis's *Bud, Not Buddy* (2000) that did not explore growing up at its core.

What makes the plots of Rowling's books so riveting to young readers may have to do with the most powerful tradition in children's literature of all: the education of the hero in fairy tales. Heroes such as Cinderella, the Ugly Duckling, Hansel and Gretel, and Little Red Riding Hood, as well as their similar counterparts in other cultures, follow much the same path. First, they start off in an ordinary world, but they quickly move into an enchanted world. Hansel and Gretel get lost in a forest and find a gingerbread house that belongs to a witch. Little Red Riding Hood also enters a forest where a clever wolf takes advantage of her trusting nature. Eventually, each hero must face trials of courage, loyalty, or ingenuity and overcome his or her weaknesses—sometimes with help from others—in order to overcome adversity. Fairy tales are short in length because they were oral tales, told to listeners in various versions, long before they were collected by writers such as the Brothers Grimm and Hans Christian Andersen. In the late nineteenth and early twentieth centuries, longer fantasy stories for young people began to appear, such as *Alice's Adventures in Wonderland* and J. M. Barrie's tremendously popular play *Peter Pan* (1904). Like fairy tales, these used enchantment as a means to move the story along. The characters in the story did not really follow the hero's path. Alice is still the same Alice, even after she falls down the rabbit hole. An exception is Carlo Collodi's *Pinocchio* (1892), who finds the qualities within himself, step-by-step, to become a real boy. *Pinocchio* has enchantment, even a fairy that guides him; it is essentially a hero's tale.

From the late 1930s on, authors of some of the great English fantasies for young people combined both fairy tales and the hero's progress into book-length fantasies for young people. In J.R.R. Tolkien's novel *The Hobbit* (1937), shy Bilbo Baggins finds himself called upon to do great deeds in a fantasy world, and he learns to be heroic in the process. In T.H. White's *The Sword in the Stone* (1939), bumbling Wart is taught by trial-and-error how to act and think like a hero by Merlyn the wizard.

Harry Potter falls into this category of writing: the fairy-tale fantasy of a hero's journey. Moreover, young readers fall deeply under Rowling's spell because the age-old elements of enchantment, dark forces, cruel relatives, and a noble main character that make fairy tales so appealing are present in the Harry Potter books. One of the first things we learn about Harry is that the Dursleys are not his real parents; they are wicked stepparents. Actually, the Dursleys are not wicked so much as they are insensitive and stupid. They refuse to recognize any other world except their ordinary one, or to acknowledge that Harry is special. Many fairy-tale characters live like Cinderella in cruel families who fail to appreciate them. This strikes a chord with many children who might like to think that the parents they live with are not their real parents.

There is also a grand secret—another key element in fairy tales—about Harry's family. His parents were sorcerers, and now, willing or not, he must live up to his birthright. Almost the same secret drives all the Star Wars movies. Luke Skywalker believes he is just a farmer who lives with his aunt and uncle. Little does he know that a mighty force for evil is headed his way. He has warrior blood in him and must heed the call to duty and adventure. Harry is also on a quest to find out more about his birth.

Before the last book was published, Rowling laughed at the popular question, Will it turn out that Voldemort is Harry's father? She responds, "No! He is NOT going to turn out to be Darth Vader."[17]

Unfortunately for Harry, he seems unfit for the job he is called upon to do, which is a big handicap shared by most fairy-tale heroes. He is meek, skinny, and wears glasses. His spoiled cousin Dudley picks on him, the way Cinderella's spoiled stepsisters ridicule her. Harry seems powerless. Many children also feel this way themselves at times. Things do not improve much for Harry when he arrives at Hogwarts. Even though he belongs at Hogwarts because he is the son of famous and admired sorcerers, other students all seem to know more than he does. Worse, a bully hounds him, and a teacher takes a very unfair disliking to him. Is there any hope for Harry?

Yes, there is, because in fairy tales, heroes who face up to life's challenges are rewarded in the end. Readers, both children and adults, like to read about characters who take action, characters we can admire. We also like characters who face struggles and hardships, and wonder if they will persevere. Harry faces many challenges and obstacles. Charles Taylor wrote on Salon.com:

> [Harry] is an outsider, one who, like many other outsiders in kids' literature, learns to value the things that have always made him feel separate from the people around him, and who also learns that the means of escape from his solitary existence has been within him all along. The book is a dream of belonging, and of discovering and self-sufficiency and courage."[18]

Perhaps Harry will emerge victorious as he struggles to gain mastery over himself, over his powers, and one day even over his enemy, Lord Voldemort. That would be a fairy-tale ending.

What will happen after Harry Potter? To the disappointment of many fans, J.K. Rowling says she will not write an eighth Harry Potter book, but she might publish an encyclopedia of the Harry Potter world, which would include her unpublished material and notes. She would give the profits from this book to a charity. In 2006, she revealed she had also completed a few short stories and a "political fairy story" aimed toward younger readers. On her Web site, she remains evasive about her plans: "There are things languishing in various drawers that I might return to, but I might write something completely different. I really don't know."[19]

Whatever she does next, Rowling has done something remarkable: She has turned millions of young readers on to reading, and she created a character who her readers will not forget. Rowling is proof that perseverance, dreaming, and dedication can pay off.

CHRONOLOGY

1965 On July 31, Joanne Rowling is born at Chipping Sodbury General Hospital in Gloucestershire, England.

1971 Family moves from Yate to Winterbourne, near Bristol; she and her younger sister Di play with an adventurous brother and sister whose last name is Potter.

1974 Rowling family moves to Tutshill, near Chepstow in Wales, on the edge of the Forest of Dean; begins to collect novels by her favorite children's authors.

1976 Enrolls at Wyedean Comprehensive; best friend Sean Harris provides the model for Ron Weasley.

1980 Rowling's mother is diagnosed with multiple sclerosis.

1982 Becomes head girl, or lead pupil, at Wyedean Comprehensive.

1983 Enrolls at University of Exeter; studies French and classics.

1985 Spends one year in Paris as teaching assistant as part of degree.

1987 Graduates from Exeter, then works briefly as a research assistant for Amnesty International; writes during lunch hours in pubs and cafés.

1988 Employed as secretary in Manchester.

1990 During long train ride from Manchester to London, suddenly imagines boy who is a wizard but he does not know it; mother dies at age 45 from multiple sclerosis.

1991 Teaches English as a foreign language in Oporto, Portugal; writes 10 different first chapters for *Harry Potter and the Philosopher's Stone*.

1992 Marries Portuguese television journalist.

1993 Gives birth to daughter, Jessica; divorces; returns to Britain with her daughter and settles in Edinburgh, Scotland, to be near her sister.

1994 Struggles to make ends meet as single parent who cannot find a job that pays well enough to provide daycare for her daughter; continues to work on Harry Potter manuscript whenever she can during the day, and at night.

1995 Sends finished manuscript to two agents and one publisher.

1996 Works as French teacher while she waits to hear about her manuscript.

1997 Scottish Arts Council gives her a large grant to continue writing; *Harry Potter and the Philosopher's Stone* is published in Britain; Scholastic purchases U.S. rights.

1998 *Harry Potter and the Chamber of Secrets* is published in Britain.

1999 *Harry Potter and the Prisoner of Azkaban* is published in Britain, becoming the No. 1 bestseller; Harry Potter books are also the top three titles on the *New York Times* fiction bestseller list.

2000 Makes *Forbes* magazine's annual Celebrity 100 list as the twenty-fourth-highest celebrity earner in the world; *Harry Potter and the Goblet of Fire* is published both in Britain and the United States at the same time.

2001 Warner Bros. releases the movie *Harry Potter and the Sorcerer's Stone.*

2002 Warner Bros. releases the second Harry Potter movie, *Harry Potter and the Chamber of Secrets.*

2003 Preorders for the book *Harry Potter and the Order of the Phoenix* make it Amazon's No. 1 bestseller five months before its June 21 publishing date.

2004 Film *Harry Potter and the Prisoner of Azkaban* is released.

2005 *Harry Potter and the Half-Blood Prince* is published; the film *Harry Potter and the Goblet of Fire* is released.

2007 *Harry Potter and the Deathly Hallows* is published.

NOTES

Chapter 1

1 Bernard Weinraub. "Harry Potter Book Becoming a Publishing Phenomenon." *The New York Times* (July 3, 2000). www.nytimes.com/library/books/070300potter-parties.html.

2 Ibid.

3 Ibid.

4 Doreen Carvajal. "Booksellers Grab a Young Wizard's Cloaktails." *The New York Times* (February 28, 2000). www.nytimes.com/library/books/022800potter-book.html.

5 "Potter 'Is Fastest-Selling Book Ever.'" BBC News (June 22, 2003). http://news.bbc.co.uk/1/hi/entertainment/arts/3005862.stm.

6 "Potter Rules in Bookstores!" Time for Kids News. http://www.timeforkids.com/TFK/news/story/0,6260,460486,00.html.

Chapter 2

1 J. K. Rowling. "The Not Especially Fascinating Life of J.K. Rowling." Cliphoto.com. www.cliphoto.com/potter/rowling.htm.

2 Kenneth Grahame, *A Wind in the Willows*. New York: Signet, 2004:5.

3 Ibid.

4 Stephen Fry. "J.K. Rowling and Stephen Fry Interview Transcript." BBC Radio 4 (December 10, 2005). http://www.mugglenet.com/jkr/interviews/bbc4.shtml.

5 J.K. Rowling, *Harry Potter and the Sorcer's Stone*, New York: Scholastic, 1998: p.105.

6 Rowling. "The Not Especially Fascinating Life of J.K. Rowling." www.cliphoto.com/potter/rowling.htm.

7 "J.K. Rowling at the Edinburgh International Book Festival," http://www.jkrowling.com/textonly/en/news_view.cfm?id=80.

8 "Transcript of J.K. Rowling's Live Interview on Scholastic.com." October 16, 2000 Book Festival. http://www.scholastic.com/harrypotter/books/author/interview2.htm.

9 Fry, "J.K. Rowling and Stephen Fry Interview Transcript." http://www.mugglenet.com/jkr/interviews/bbc4.shtml.

10 "Biography," J.K. Rowling Official Site, http://www.jkrowling.com/textonly/en/biography.cfm.

11 Ibid.

12 "Transcript of J.K. Rowling's Live Interview on Scholastic.com," http://www.scholastic.

com/harrypotter/books/author/
interview2.htm.

Chapter 3

1 "Biography," J.K. Rowling Official Site. http://www.jkrowling.com/textonly/en/biography.cfm.

2 "Virtual Tour," University of Exeter, http://www.exeter.ac.uk/virtualtours/streathambroadband/index.shtml.

3 "Transcript of J.K. Rowling's Live Interview on Scholastic.com." October 16, 2000 Book Festival. http://www.scholastic.com/harrypotter/books/author/interview2.htm.

4 "Biography," J.K. Rowling Official Site. http://www.jkrowling.com/textonly/en/biography.cfm.

5 Ibid.

6 Ibid.

7 Fry, "J.K. Rowling and Stephen Fry Interview Transcript." BBC Radio 4 (December 10, 2005). http://www.mugglenet.com/jkr/interviews/bbc4.shtml.

8 "Biography," J.K. Rowling Official Site. http://www.jkrowling.com/textonly/en/biography.cfm.

9 Ibid.

10 Geordie Greig. "There Would Be so Much to Tell Her." *The Telegraph* (November 1, 2006). http://www.telegraph.co.uk/news/main.jhtml?xml=/news/2006/01/10/nrowl110.xml.

Chapter 4

1 Matt Seaton. "If I Could Talk to My Mum Again I'd Tell Her I Had a Daughter—and I Wrote Some Books and Guess What Happened?" *The Guardian* (April 18, 2001). http://books.guardian.co.uk/departments/childrenandteens/story/0,6000,474412,00.html.

2 Greig, "There Would Be so Much to Tell Her." *The Telegraph* (November 1, 2006). http://www.telegraph.co.uk/news/main.jhtml?xml=/news/2006/01/10/nrowl110.xml.

3 Simone Hattenstone. "Harry, Jessie and Me." *The Guardian* (July 8, 2000). http://books.guardian.co.uk/departments/childrenandteens/story/0,6000,340844,00.html.

4 Seaton, "If I Could Talk to My Mum Again I'd Tell Her I Had a Daughter—and I Wrote Some Books and Guess What Happened?", http://books.guardian.co.uk/departments/childrenandteens/story/0,6000,474412,00.html.

5 "Transcript of J.K. Rowling's Live Interview on Scholastic.com." October 16, 2000 Book Festival. http://www.scholastic.com/harrypotter/books/author/interview2.htm.

6 Seaton, "If I Could Talk to My Mum Again I'd Tell Her I Had a Daughter—and I Wrote Some Books and Guess What Happened?" http://books.guardian.co.uk/

departments/childrenandteens/
story/0,6000,474412,00.html.

Chapter 5

1 Arthur A. Levine. "Why I Paid
So Much for a Children's Book"
The New York Times (October 13,
1999). www.nytimes.com/library/
financial/101399manage-levine.
html.

2 Peter H. Gleick. "Harry Potter,
Minus a Certain Flavour."
The New York Times (July 10,
2000). www.nytimes.com/
books/00/07/23/specials/rowling-
gleick.html.

3 "Transcript of J.K. Rowling's
Live Interview on Scholastic.
com." October 16, 2000 Book
Festival. http://www.scholastic.
com/harrypotter/books/author/
interview2.htm.

Chapter 6

1 Fry, "J.K. Rowling and Stephen
Fry Interview Transcript."
http://www.mugglenet.com/jkr/
interviews/bbc4.shtml.

2 "Potter's Author's Content
Warning." BBC News
(September 27, 2000). www.
cesnur.org/recens/potter_062.htm.

3 Ibid.

4 Ibid.

5 Anthony Holden. "Why Harry
Potter Doesn't Cast a Spell
Over Me." *The Observer*
(June 25, 2000). http://observer.
guardian.co.uk/review/
story/0,6903,335923,00.html.

6 Janet Maslin. "At Last, the Wizard
Gets Back to School." *The New
York Times* (July 10, 2000).

www.nytimes.com/library/books/
071000rowling-book-review.html.

7 "Transcript of J.K. Rowling's
Interview at the Edinburgh
International Book Festival."
http://www.scholastic.com/
harrypotter/authortranscript4.htm.

8 Kera Bolonick. "A List of Their
Own." Salon.com (August 16,
2000). www.salon.com/mwt/
feature/2000/08/16/bestseller/
index.html.

9 Ibid.

10 "J.K. Rowling at the Edinburgh
International Book Festival,"
http://www.jkrowling.com/
textonly/en/news_view.cfm?id=80.

Chapter 7

1 Hattenstone, "Harry, Jessie
and Me." *The Guardian*
(July 8, 2000). http://books.
guardian.co.uk/departments/
childrenandteens/story/0,6
000,340844,00.html.

2 "Mugglenet and the Leaky
Cauldron Interview J.K.
Rowling." Mugglenet.com.
http://www.mugglenet.com/
jkrinterview3.shtml.

3 "Transcript of J.K. Rowling's
Live Interview on Scholastic.
com." October 16, 2000 Book
Festival. http://www.scholastic.
com/harrypotter/books/author/
interview2.htm.

4 John Leonard. "Nobody Expects
the Inquisition." Book Review:
"Harry Potter and the Order of the
Phoenix." *New York Times Book
Review* (July 13, 2003): p. 13.

5 "Mugglenet and the Leaky
Cauldron Interview J.K. Rowling."

http://www.mugglenet.com/
jkrinterview.shtml.

6 Liesl Schillinger, "Her Dark
Materials." Book Review: "Harry
Potter and the Half-Blood Prince,"
The New York Times Book Review
(July 31, 2005): p. 12(L).

Chapter 8

1 "Transcript of J.K. Rowling's
Live Interview on Scholastic.
com." October 16, 2000 Book
Festival. http://www.scholastic.
com/harrypotter/books/author/
interview2.htm.

2 "Mugglenet and the
Leaky Cauldron Interview
J.K. Rowling." Mugglenet.com.
http://www.mugglenet.com/
jkrinterview.shtml.

3 Leonard, "Nobody Expects the
Inquisition."

4 Schillinger, "Her Dark Materials."
Book Review: "Harry Potter and
the Half-Blood Prince," *The New
York Times Book Review* (July 31,
2005): p. 12(L).

5 "J.K. Rowling at the Edinburgh
International Book Festival,"
http://www.jkrowling.com/
textonly/en/news_view.cfm?id=80.

6 Ibid.

7 "Mugglenet and the Leaky
Cauldron Interview J.K.
Rowling." http://www.mugglenet.
com/jkrinterview1.shtml.

8 Deirdre Donahue. "When Jim
Dale Speaks, People Listen to
'Potter.'" *USA Today* (July 14,
2005). http://www.usatoday.com/
life/books/news/2005-07-14-dale-
potter-audiobooks_x.htm.

9 "Transcript of J.K. Rowling's
Live Interview on Scholastic.
com." http://www.scholastic.
com/harrypotter/books/author/
interview2.htm.

10 "Mugglenet and the Leaky
Cauldron Interview J.K.
Rowling." http://www.mugglenet.
com/jkrinterview1.shtml.

11 "Transcript of J.K. Rowling's
Live Interview on Scholastic.
com." http://www.scholastic.
com/harrypotter/books/author/
interview2.htm.

12 Ibid.

13 "Mugglenet and the Leaky
Cauldron Interview J.K.
Rowling." http://www.mugglenet.
com/jkrinterview.shtml.

14 "Diary." J.K. Rowling Official
Site. Archived at http://www.
hp-lexicon.org/about/sources/jkr.
com/jkr-com-diary.html.

Chapter 9

1 Alan Cowell. "The Subtlety
of Hogwarts? Give a Wizard a
Break!" *The New York Times*
(August 12, 2000). www.nytimes.
com/library/books/081200anti-
potter.html.

2 Quoted in Cowell, "The Subtlety
of Hogwarts?"

3 Ibid.

4 William Safire. "Besotted With
Potter." *The New York Times*
(January 27, 2000). www.nytimes.
com/library/opinion/safire/
012700safi.html.

5 Lindy Beam. "What Shall
We Do with Harry?" Minnesota
Family Council. http://www.mfc.
org/contents/article.cfm?id=378.

6 Ben Roy. "Wiccans Dispute Potter Claims." *Citizen Online-Newfound Area Bureau* (October 26, 2000). www.cesnur.org/recens/potter_069.htm.

7 Fry, "J.K. Rowling and Stephen Fry Interview Transcript." BBC Radio 4 (December 10, 2005). http://www.mugglenet.com/jkr/interviews/bbc4.shtml.

8 Ibid.

9 Judy Blume. "Is Harry Potter Evil?" *New York Times* (October 22, 1999). www.judyblume.com/censorship/potter.php.

10 Jodi Wilgoren. "Don't Give Us Little Wizards, the Anti-Potter Parents Cry." *New York Times* (November 1, 1999). www.nytimes.com/library/books/110199harry-potter.html.

11 "Banned Books Week." J.K. Rowling Official Site. http://www.jkrowling.com/textonly/en/news_view.cfm?id=95.

12 Leonard, "Nobody Expects the Inquisition."

13 Levine, "Why I Paid So Much for a Children's Book."

14 A.O. Scott. "Harry Potter Is the New Star Wars." The Book Club, *Slate* (August 23, 1999). http://www.slate.com/id/2000111/entry/1003472/.

15 David D. Kirkpatrick. "Harry Potter Magic Halts Bedtime for Youngsters." *New York Times* (July 9, 2000). www.nytimes.com/library/books/070900potter-goblet.html.

16 Ibid.

17 Fry, "J.K. Rowling and Stephen Fry Interview Transcript." http://www.mugglenet.com/jkr/interviews/bbc4.shtml.

18 Charles Taylor. "This Sorcery Isn't Just for Kids." Salon.com (March 31, 1999). www.salon.com/mwt/feature/1999/03/cov_31featurea2.html.

19 "F.A.Q." J.K. Rowling Official Site. http://www.jkrowling.com/textonly/en/faq_view.cfm?id=107.

WORKS BY J.K. ROWLING

1997 *Harry Potter and the Philosopher's Stone* (called *Harry Potter and the Sorcer's Stone* in the United States)

1998 *Harry Potter and the Chamber of Secrets*

1999 *Harry Potter and the Prisoner of Azkaban*

2000 *Harry Potter and the Goblet of Fire*

2001 *Harry Potter Schoolbooks: Fantastic Beasts and Where to Find Them; Quidditch Through the Ages* (Benefit for the Comic Relief Foundation)

2003 *Harry Potter and the Order of the Phoenix*

2005 *Harry Potter and the Half-Blood Prince*

2007 *Harry Potter and the Deathly Hallows*

POPULAR BOOKS

HARRY POTTER AND THE CHAMBER OF SECRETS

The much-anticipated sequel to *Harry Potter and the Sorcerer's Stone*. Happy to be back at school at Hogwarts after spending a terrible summer with the Dursleys, Harry is soon faced with more adventure and mystery. It seems as though his classmate Draco Malfoy is out to get him. Harry also hears frightening voices that whisper from the walls. Harry, Hermione, and Ron use their wizardly skills to solve a 50-year-old mystery.

HARRY POTTER AND THE DEATHLY HALLOWS

In the climatic end to the series, Rowling immerses her audience in suspense and conflict as Harry and his friends battle Voldemort for the last time. After leaving Hogwarts with Ron and Hermione, Harry embarks on a mission to stop Voldemort forever but finds himself drawn to the mystery of the Deathly Hallows. As beloved heroes and villains fight for their lives and dreams, the lingering questions surrounding the connection between two of the greatest wizards in history are finally answered. The book's pace is fast and dangerous as Harry and Voldemort race to battle each twist and turn on the path to destroy each other, leading to a surprising, dramatic end.

HARRY POTTER AND THE GOBLET OF FIRE

With this fourth installment, the Harry Potter books take a darker turn. For a while, Harry tries to forget about Lord Voldemort while he, Ron, and Hermione attend the thrilling international Quidditch match. Then he finds out that the Hogwarts school will compete against two rival magicians' schools in a Triwizard event. In this suspenseful installment, there are many hair-raising moments, where readers fear for Harry's life. Rowling leaves several plot strands open, to be continued in Book 5.

HARRY POTTER AND THE HALF-BLOOD PRINCE

The long-awaited, eagerly anticipated sixth book in the series. This book is much darker and more sophisticated, and the reader learns important revelations. In *Harry Potter and the Half-Blood Prince*, no one and nothing is safe, including preconceived notions of good and evil and of right and wrong. Rowling has raised the stakes with each book. A series that began as an exciting adventure filled with magic and discovery has become a dark and deadly war zone.

HARRY POTTER AND THE ORDER OF THE PHOENIX

As his fifth year at Hogwarts School of Witchcraft and Wizardry, Harry is now 15 years old, a teenager with fits of rage, a major crush, and a desire to rebel. The fifth book is much darker, and also more of a coming-of-age novel. Harry faces an overwhelming course load as the fifth-year students prepare for their examinations, disappointing changes in the Gryffindor Quidditch team lineup, and a new Defense Against the Dark Arts teacher. He also has vivid dreams about long hallways and closed doors, and increasing pain in his lightning-shaped scar. Harry confronts death again, and he also learns a startling prophecy.

HARRY POTTER AND THE PRISONER OF AZKABAN

Harry is 13 years old in the third Harry Potter book. He is home again for the summer, ahd he hates his time with the Dursleys. After a hilarious incident in which he inflates Aunt Marge, Harry returns to Hogwarts where he is told that the dangerous Sirius Black has escaped from the prison of Azkaban and is on the hunt for Harry. Rowling has created another suspenseful mystery.

HARRY POTTER AND THE SORCERER'S STONE

This first book in the series introduces Harry, whose parents were killed by the evil Lord Voldemort. Voldemort also attempted to kill Harry, who was only an infant, but he miraculously survived. Now age 11, Harry lives under the stairs of a boring Muggle family who does not treat him well. One day, he receives a mysterious letter that tells him that he has been accepted at Hogwarts School of Witchcraft and Wizardry. The adventures soon begin: magical, humorous, and suspenseful.

POPULAR CHARACTERS

SIRIUS BLACK

The most infamous prisoner to ever be held at Azkaban, the wizards' prison, Black escapes from Azkaban at the beginning of *Harry Potter and the Prisoner of Azkaban*. Black was accused of murdering 13 people with a single curse. He was the best friend of James Potter, Harry's dad.

ALBUS DUMBLEDORE

Albus Dumbledore is the Headmaster at Hogwarts School, the most powerful wizard of all. He has long white hair, a white beard, and he dresses in long green or red robes. He is highly educated, peace-loving, and wise. Dark wizards fear his power, even though he uses it in the cause of good.

HERMIONE GRANGER

Hermione, friend of both Ron and Harry, is at the top of her class, even though her parents are Muggles. She is clever and excels at solving problems, yet she is sympathetic, too. By her toughness and fairness, she inspires others.

RUBEUS HAGRID

Hagrid is the gamekeeper at Hogwarts School. He is a half-giant with long black hair and warm, good-natured eyes who is well liked by the students. Hagrid has a special affection for creatures like dragons, monsters of all sorts, and centaurs.

DRACO MALFOY

Draco is cunning and jealous, and he and Harry despise each other. He loves nothing more than to see Harry and his friends fail, and he tries to make that happen whenever he can.

LUCIUS MALFOY

Draco Malfoy's father, Lucius, is the head of a pureblood wizarding family. He was once governor of the Hogwarts School, but he was fired when he threatened the families of the other governors so they would suspend Headmaster Albus Dumbledore.

MINERVA MCGONAGALL

Minerva McGonagall is the Deputy Headmistress of Hogwarts, head of the Gryffindor house, and teacher of Transfiguration. She has the ability to transform herself into many animals, although she prefers to change into a cat because she possesses the traits of one.

MOONY (REMUS LUPIN)

Professor of Defense Against the Dark Arts, who first appears in *Harry Potter and the Prisoner of Azkaban.* Moony is a werewolf. He is also a more powerful wizard than he lets on.

HARRY POTTER

Harry Potter, the hero of the series, is a boy with black hair, green eyes framed by a pair of glasses, and a lightening-shaped scar on his forehead. His parents were killed during a battle of magic against the evil wizard Lord Voldemort, and he has been nicknamed "The Boy Who Lived." Harry is modest, yet loyal, courageous, and morally upright. His years at Hogwarts, as he learns to become a wizard, form the overall framework of the books.

RITA SKEETER

A relentless journalist who enters the series in *Harry Potter and the Goblet of Fire,* Skeeter causes trouble for just about everyone by writing exaggerated, untrue stories for the *Daily Prophet.*

PROFESSOR SEVERUS SNAPE

Snape teaches Potions and is the head of the Slytherin house. Snape seems to have it in for Harry, and he is fascinated by the Dark Arts. He is a former classmate and enemy of James Potter's.

LORD VOLDEMORT

Lord Voldemort is also called the Dark Lord and "You-Know-Who." A powerful magician of the Dark Magic, he is eager to wreak havoc on his enemies. Voldemort can transform himself into different creatures, and he intends to take over the world. Lord Voldemort went into hiding after he was unable to kill Harry as an infant, and he is Harry's antagonist throughout the series.

GINNY WEASLEY

The youngest child and the only girl in the Weasley family. Ginny is shy, but as the series continues, she develops into a strong character with a temper, who is loyal and warm-hearted. Ginny plays an important role in Harry Potter's life.

RONALD WEASLEY

Tall with red hair and freckles, Ron is Harry's best friend, and the sixth of seven children in his family. His brothers all did very well at Hogwarts, which casts a kind of shadow over Ron's hard-won accomplishments. He is faithful and always ready for adventure, even if he is a little clumsy.

MAJOR AWARDS

1997 *Harry Potter and the Philosopher's Stone*, winner of Nestlé Smarties Book Prize Gold Medal (9-11 years category).

1998 *Harry Potter and the Philosopher's Stone,* named British Book Awards' Children's Book of the Year and the Young Telegraph Paperback of the Year; winner of the Sheffield Children's Book Award; *Harry Potter and the Chamber of Secrets,* winner of the Nestlé Smarties Book Prize Gold Medal (9-11 years category).

1999 *Harry Potter and the Chamber of Secrets*, winner of the Scottish Arts Council Children's Book Award and named the British Book Awards' Children's Book of the Year; *Harry Potter and the Prisoner of Azkaban*, winner of the Nestlé Smarties Book Prize Gold Medal (9-11 years category) and the Whitbread Children's Book Award.

2003 *Harry Potter and the Order of the Phoenix,* named W.H. Smith People's Choice Award.

2006 *Harry Potter and the Half-Blood Prince*, named the British Book Awards' Children's Book of the Year

BIBLIOGRAPHY

Beam, Lindy. "What Shall We Do with Harry?" Minnesota Family Council. Available online. URL: www.mfc.org/contents/article. cfm?id=378.

Blume, Judy. "Is Harry Potter Evil?" *The New York Times* (October 22, 1999). Available online. URL: www.judyblume.com/censorship/ potter.php.

Bolonick, Kera. "A List of Their Own." Salon.com (August 16, 2000). Available online. URL: www.salon.com/mwt/feature/2000/08/16/ bestseller/index.html.

Carvajal, Doreen. "Booksellers Grab a Young Wizard's Cloaktails." *The New York Times* (February 28, 2000). Available online. URL: www.nytimes.com/library/books/022800potter-book.html.

————. "Children's Book Casts a Spell over Adults." *The New York Times* (April 1, 1999). Available online. URL: www.nytimes.com/library/ books/040199potter-book.html.

Cowell, Alan. "The Subtlety of Hogwarts? Give a Wizard a Break!" *The New York Times* (August 12, 2000). Available online. URL: www.nytimes.com/library/books/081200anti-potter.html.

Donahue, Deirdre. "When Jim Dale Speaks, People Listen to 'Potter.'" *USA Today* (July 14, 2005). Available online. URL: http://www. usatoday.com/life/books/news/2005-07-14-dale-potter-audiobooks_ x.htm.

Fry, Stephen. "J.K. Rowling and Stephen Fry Interview Transcript." BBC Radio 4 (December 10, 2005). Available online. URL: http:// www.mugglenet.com/jkr/interviews/bbc4.shtml.

Geordie Greig. "There Would Be So Much to Tell Her." *The Telegraph* (November 1, 2006). Available online. URL: http://www.tclcgraph. co.uk/news/main.jhtml?xml=/news/2006/01/10/nrowl110.xml.

Gleick, Peter H. "Harry Potter, Minus a Certain Flavour." *The New York Times* (July 10, 2000). Available online. URL: www.nytimes.com/ books/00/07/23/specials/rowling-gleick.html.

Hattenstone, Simone. "Harry, Jessie and Me." *The Guardian* (July 8, 2000). Available online. URL: http://books.guardian.co.uk/ departments/childrenandteens/story/0,6 000,340844,00.html.

Holden, Anthony. "Why Harry Potter Doesn't Cast a Spell over Me." *The Observer* (June 25, 2000). Available online. URL: http://observer. guardian.co.uk/review/story/0,6903,335923,00.html.

"J. K. Rowling Reveals Secrets of Her Success." *USA Today* (July 9, 2000). Available online. URL: www.usatoday.com/life/enter/books/ potter/hp03.htm.

Kirkpatrick, David D. "Harry Potter Magic Halts Bedtime for Youngsters." *The New York Times* (July 9, 2000). Available online. URL: www. nytimes.com/library/books/070900potter-goblet.html.

Leonard, John. "Nobody Expects the Inquisition." Book Review: "Harry Potter and the Order of the Phoenix." *The New York Times Book Review* (July 13, 2003): p. 13.

Levine, Arthur A. "Why I Paid So Much for a Children's Book." *The New York Times* (October 13, 1999). Available online. URL: www.nytimes. com/library/financial/101399manage-levine.html.

Maslin, Janet. "At Last, the Wizard Gets Back to School." *The New York Times* (July 10, 2000). Available online. URL: www.nytimes.com/ library/books/071000rowling-book-review.html.

"Potter 'Is Fastest-selling Book Ever'." BBC News (June 22, 2003). Available online. URL: http://news.bbc.co.uk/1/hi/entertainment/ arts/3005862.stm.

"Potter Rules in Bookstores!" Time for Kids News. Available online. URL: http://www.timeforkids.com/TFK/news/story/0,6260,460486,00.html.

"Potter's Author's Content Warning." BBC News (September 27, 2000). Available online. URL: www.cesnur.org/recens/potter_062.htm.

Rowling, J.K. "Biography." J.K. Rowling Official Site. Available online. URL: http://www.jkrowling.com/textonly/en/biography.cfm.

———. "Diary." J.K. Rowling Official Site. Available online. URL: http://www.jkrowling.com/textonly/en/.

———. "F.A.Q." J.K. Rowling Official Site. Available online. URL: http:// www.jkrowling.com/textonly/en/faq_view.cfm?id=75.

———. Interview. "Mugglenet and the Leaky Cauldron Interview J.K. Rowling." Mugglenet.com. Available online. URL: http:// www.mugglenet.com/jkrinterview.shtml.

———. Interview. "Transcript of J.K. Rowling's Live Interview on Scholastic.com." October 16, 2000, Book Festival. Available online. URL: http://www.scholastic.com/harrypotter/books/author/ interview2.htm.

Rowling, J.K. Interview. "J.K. Rowling at the Edinburgh International Book Festival." Available online. URL: http://www.jkrowling.com/textonly/en/news_view.cfm?id=80.

Rowling, J.K. "The Not Especially Fascinating Life of J.K. Rowling." Cliphoto.com. Available online. URL: www.cliphoto.com/potter/rowling.htm.

Roy, Ben. "Wiccans Dispute Potter Claims." *Citizen Online-Newfound Area Bureau* (October 26, 2000). Available online. URL: www.cesnur.org/recens/potter_069.htm.

Safire, William. "Besotted With Potter." *The New York Times* (January 27, 2000). Available online. URL: www.nytimes.com/library/opinion/safire/012700safi.html.

Schillinger, Liesl. "Her Dark Materials." Book Review: "Harry Potter and the Half-Blood Prince." *The New York Times Book Review* (July 31, 2005): p. 12(L).

Scott, A.O. "The End of Innocence." *The New York Times Magazine* (July 2, 2000). Available online. URL: www.nytimes.com/library/magazine/home/20000702mag-waywelivenow .html.

Seaton, Matt. "If I Could Talk to My Mum Again I'd Tell Her I Had a Daughter—and I Wrote Some Books and Guess What Happened?" *The Guardian* (April 18, 2001). Available online. URL: http://books.guardian.co.uk/departments/childrenandteens/story/0,6000,474412,00.html.

Taylor, Charles. "This Sorcery Isn't Just for Kids." Salon.com (March 31, 1999). Available online. URL: www.salon.com/mwt/feature/1999/03/cov_31featurea2.html.

Weinraub, Bernard. "Harry Potter Book Becoming a Publishing Phenomenon." *The New York Times* (July 3, 2000). Available online. URL: www.nytimes.com/library/books/070300potter-parties.html.

Wilgoren, Jodi. "Don't Give Us Little Wizards, the Anti-Potter Parents Cry." *The New York Times* (November 1, 1999). Available online. URL: www.nytimes.com/library/books/110199harry-potter.html.

FURTHER READING

Adler, Bill, ed. *Kids' Letters to Harry Potter from Around the World: An Unauthorized Collection.* New York: Carroll & Graf, 2001.

Boyle, Fionna. *A Muggles Guide to the Wizarding World: Exploring the Harry Potter Universe.* Toronto: ECW Press, 2004.

Colbert, David. *The Magical Worlds of Harry Potter.* New York: Berkeley Books, 2002.

Fraser, Lindsey. *Conversations with J.K. Rowling.* New York: Scholastic, 2001.

Web Sites

American Library Association: Banned Books Week
http://www.ala.org/ala/oif/bannedbooksweek/bannedbooksweek.htm

Harry Potter Lexicon
http://www.hp-lexicon.org/index-2.html

J.K. Rowling Official Site
http://www.jkrowling.com/

Kidsreads.com Presents Harry Potter
http://www.kidsreads.com/harrypotter/jkrowling.html

Kids Scholastic: Harry Potter
http://www.scholastic.com/harrypotter/author/

PICTURE CREDITS

INDEX

Alexander, Lloyd, 15
Alice's Adventures in Wonderland
  (Carroll), 107, 110
Amazon.com, 12, 62
American Library Association
  (ALA), 105
American Way of Death, An
  (Mitford), 29
Amnesty International, 33
Andersen, Hans Christian, 110
Anelli, Melissa, 97
Arantes, Jessica (daughter), 43,
  46–47, 79
Arantes, Jorge (ex-husband), 43, 48
Are You There God? It's Me,
  Margaret (Blume), 105
audiobooks, 17, 46–47, 94
Austen, Jane, 78

Ballet Shoes (Streatfeild), 24
Barnes & Noble, 18, 89
Barrie, J.M., 110
bestseller lists, children's, 77–78
birth of J.K. Rowling, 22
Bloom, Harold, 102
Bloomsbury Publishing, 53–54, 62
Blume, Judy, 105
Bologna Book Fair (Italy), 56
books, recommended (list), 24
Books of Magic (Gaiman), 36
British Smarties Book Prize, 71
Brothers Grimm, 110
Bucharest, Romania, 82
Bud, Not Buddy (Curtis), 110

Carroll, Lewis, 107
charities, 82–83, 113
Charlotte's Web (E.B. White), 15

childhood of J.K. Rowling, 22
Chocolate War, The (Cormier),
  109
Christopher Little Literary Agency,
  48–49, 51–52, 53–54
Chronicles of Narnia (Lewis), 15, 25,
  37, 107
Chronicles of Prydian (Alexander),
  15
Cleary, Beverly, 62
Coca-Cola, 84
Collodi, Carlo, 110
Columbus, Chris, 84
Comic Relief, 82
Cormier, Robert, 109
Cotler, Joanna, 77
critical reviews of Potter series, 73,
  80, 85, 88, 92–93, 101–103
Cuarôn, Alfonso, 84
Cunningham, Barry, 54
Curtis, Christopher Paul, 110

Dale, Jim, 17, 46–47, 94
death of mother, 38–39, 41–42
depression, 46–47
devil-may-care attitude, 32
Ditlow, Tim, 94
divorce, 43
Doctor of Laws (LLD) degree
  (honorary), 83
dreaming of Harry, 16, 34–37

Edinburgh, Scotland, 44–45
education, 26, 27, 32–33
Elephant House Café (Edinburgh),
  44–45
Everall, Annie, 103
Exeter, University of, 32–33

fairy tales, 110

fans, Potter, 14, 62–63, 96–97

Fantastic Beasts and Where to Find Them (booklet), 82

Fielding, Helen, 82

films of Potter books, 83–84, 88

Forest of Dean, Royal, 25

Fry, Stephen, 71

Gaiman, Neil, 36

Gallico, Paul , 24

Gammage Cup, The (Kendall), 70

Girl of the Limberlost (Stratten-Porter), 24

Gleik, Peter, 58

Goosebumps series (Stine), 68

Goudge, Elizabeth, 23

Grahame, Kenneth, 22, 25

Gratz, Wendi, 16

Greenpeace, 61

Grimm, Brothers, 110

Guinness World Records, 88

Harris, Sean, 28–29

Harry Potter
  autobiographical nature of, 37–38
  boarding school for, 27, 37
  insecurity of, 106, 112
  in Rowling's dreams, 16, 34–37
  spiritual ancestor of, 36

Harry Potter and the Chamber of Secrets, 61, 62–64

Harry Potter and the Deathly Hallows, 18–19, 88–89, 98–99

Harry Potter and the Goblet of Fire
  content of, 74–77
  film of, 84
  popularity of, 11–12, 17, 18, 89
  problems with, 73–74
  tribute to Mitford in, 29

Harry Potter and the Half-Blood Prince, 18, 61, 85, 88, 96

Harry Potter and the Order of the Phoenix, 17–18, 84–87

Harry Potter and the Philosopher's Stone (UK). *See Harry Potter and the Sorcerer's Stone*

Harry Potter and the Prisoner of Azkaban, 47, 67, 69, 84

Harry Potter and the Sorcerer's Stone
  Americanization of, 57–60
  bestseller status of, 62, 64
  content of, 54–56, 109
  excerpt on death of parents, 42–43
  first book of series, 13, 19, 54
  Forbidden Forest and, 25–26
  rejections of by publishers, 53
  submittal of first draft, 48–49
  sudden wealth and, 81–82

Harry Potter IV (CD), 17

Harry Potter Withdrawal Club, 15

Haven Foundation, 82

Hermione Granger
  autobiographical nature of, 26
  in defiance of elves, 29

Hogwarts Express, 10, 13–15

Holden, Anthony, 73

I Capture the Castle (Smith), 24, 69

Internet. *See* Web sites

interviews, 71–72

Irving, John, 82, 98

Jacobs, Michael, 12

Jacques, Brian, 15

Joanna Cotler Books (HarperCollins Children's), 77

Jones, Diana Wynne, 36

Kendall, Carol, 70

King, Stephen, 82, 98

King's Cross Station, 37

Kipling, Rudyard, 109

Klein, Richard, 12

Kloves, Steve, 84

Korves, Alexandra and Douglas, 18

Le Guin, Ursula K., 107
Legend of Rah and the Muggles (Stouffer), 70
Leonard, John, 85, 92, 106
Levine, Arthur A., 56, 106
Lewis, C.S., 15, 25, 37, 107
library fines, 32–33
Little White Horse, The (Goudge), 23–24

Manxmouse (Gallico), 24
Marcus, Barbara, 78
marriages, 43, 78
Maslin, Janet, 76
McCrum, Robert, 102
Mitford, Jessica, 28, 29, 32
Monty Python, 93
muggles, origin of, 70
Multiple Sclerosis Society of Scotland, 82
Murphy, Jill, 36
Murray, David Gordon (son), 78
Murray, Mackenzie (daughter), 78, 85–86
Murray, Neil (second husband), 78

National Council for One Parent Families (Britain), 82
National Wildlife Federation, 61
Nesbit, E., 25
New York Times bestseller list, 71, 77–78
Newbery award for children's literature, 109
Newell, Mike, 84
Nicholson's Café (Edinburgh), 44–45
"Not Especially Fascinating Life of J.K. Rowling, The," 22

Observer, The, 73
Officer of the Order of the British Empire, 71
Once and Future King, The (T.H. White), 36
Oporto, Portugal, 40, 41–42

paper, recycled, 61
Peck, Richard, 110
Peter Pan (Barrie), 110
Pinocchio (Collodi), 110
Potter, Harry. *See* Harry Potter
Potter, Ian and Vicki, 23
Potter series. *See also* critical reviews of Potter series; Pottermania
　Americanization of, 57–60
　backstories of characters, 93–94
　bestseller status of, 62, 64, 77–78, 88–89
　challenges to, 104–106
　in defense of, 105
　films of, 83–84, 88
　growth of children's book sales and, 68
　inhabitants of, 92
　key elements in, 110–112
　plotting of, 91–92
　as publishing phenomenon, 64–65, 67–68
　translations of, 67, 88
Pottermania, 11–12, 17–19, 62–65, 88–89
privacy, loss of, 72, 77–79
publicity campaigns, 98–99

Quidditch Through the Ages (booklet), 82

Radcliffe, Daniel, 35
Radio City Music Hall, 82
Raincoast Books (Canada), 61, 96
Ramona series (Cleary), 62
Reading Is Fundamental (charity), 84
Real Canadian Superstore, 96
recommended books (list), 24
recycled paper, 61
Redwall series (Jacques), 15, 69
reviews of Potter series. *See* critical reviews of Potter series
Riggio, Steve, 107
Ron Weasley, model for, 28

Rowling, Anne (mother)
  birth of J.K. (Joanne) and Di, 22
  courtship of, 21
  death of, 38–39, 41–42
  multiple sclerosis and, 29
Rowling, Di (sister), 22–23, 44–45, 48
Rowling, Peter (father), 21–22

Safire, William, 102
Schillinger, Liesl, 88, 92
Scholastic Children's Book Group, 78
Scholastic Press, 56, 61, 69, 70
Scott, A.O., 106
Scottish Arts Council, 56
Shulz, Louis, 11
Simpsons, The, 86
Smith, Delia, 82
Smith, Dodie, 24
socialism, 29
Spartz, Emerson, 97
Spielberg, Steven, 84
St. Martin's Press, 69
Stalky & Co. (Kipling), 109
Star Wars movies, 111
Stine, R.L., 68
Story of the Treasure Seekers, The (Nesbit), 25
Stouffer, Nancy K., 70
Stratten-Porter, Gene, 24
Streatfeild, Noel, 24
style, writing, 91–93
Sword in the Stone, The (T.H. White), 111

Tales of Fourth Grade Nothing (Blume), 105
Taylor, Charles, 112
Taylor, Thomas, 60
teaching French in Edinburgh, 52–53
themes of other authors, 36
translations, 67, 88

Voldemort, 54–56

wealth of J.K. Rowling, 81–83
Web sites
  by fans, 97
  official, 18–19, 28, 96–97, 113
  on progress of seventh (final) book, 98
Whitbread Children's Book of the Year award, 71
White, E.B., 15
White, T.H., 36, 111
Wind in the Willows (Grahame), 22, 25
Witch Week (Jones), 36
Wizard of Earthsea (Le Guin), 107
Worst Witch series (Murphy), 36
Wouldbegoods, The (Nesbit), 25
writer's block, 60–61
writing, early influences on, 22–25
Wyedean Comprehensive day school, 27, 32

Year Down Yonder, A (Peck), 110

ABOUT THE AUTHOR

AMY SICKELS lives in New York City. She received her MFA from Penn State University, and she has published stories and essays in literary journals, including *The Greensboro Review* and *The Madison Review*.